T0305416

TRANSPORT TRUTHS

Urban Transport Futures

Series Editor: **William Riggs**,
University of San Francisco, US

This series explores how changing technologies and transport
innovations are influencing possibilities for our cities and city futures
across the globe. It provides academics, policy makers and city planners
with the insights and tools to ensure that future transport systems
are sustainable, equitable and inclusive.

Find out more at:
bristoluniversitypress.co.uk/urban-transport-futures

TRANSPORT TRUTHS

Planning Methods and Ethics for Global Futures

Greg P. Griffin

BRISTOL
UNIVERSITY
PRESS

First published in Great Britain in 2025 by

Bristol University Press
University of Bristol
1–9 Old Park Hill
Bristol
BS2 8BB
UK
t: +44 (0)117 374 6645
e: bup-info@bristol.ac.uk

Details of international sales and distribution partners are available at bristoluniversitypress.co.uk

© Bristol University Press 2025

British Library Cataloguing in Publication Data
A catalogue record for this book is available from the British Library

ISBN 978-1-5292-2745-1 hardcover
ISBN 978-1-5292-2747-5 ePub
ISBN 978-1-5292-2748-2 ePdf

Cover design: Liam Roberts Design
Front cover image: Stocksy/Dylan M. Howell Photography
Bristol University Press uses environmentally responsible print partners.
Printed and bound in Great Britain by CPI Group (UK) Ltd, Croydon, CR0 4YY

FSC
www.fsc.org
MIX
Paper | Supporting
responsible forestry
FSC® C013604

Contents

Series Editor Preface

William Riggs
(University of San Francisco, US)

In a world that is increasingly reliant on interconnected transportation systems to provide lifelines for cities and regions, how can we find truth? Our transportation systems are not just about moving people and goods from one place to another; they are complex sociotechnical ensembles that shape, and are shaped by, the societies they serve. And in *Transport Truths: Planning Methods and Ethics for Global Futures*, Greg Griffin explores the methods that underpin how we plan for transport, highlighting the need for a comprehensive approach to address modern challenges.

As an important entry in the *Transport Futures* series at Bristol University Press, the book emerges from a realization that traditional approaches to transport planning often fall short in addressing the wicked challenges of our time. The need for sustainable, equitable, and efficient transport systems has never been more pressing, yet the path to achieving these goals is fraught with complexities and contradictions. By integrating insights from diverse disciplines and employing a critical realist perspective, Griffin provides a comprehensive framework for understanding and addressing these multifaceted challenges.

For example, quantitative methods such as statistical analysis and traffic modeling provide valuable data on transport patterns and trends. However, they often fail to capture the nuances of individual experiences and the broader social context. Similarly, qualitative methods, such as interviews and focus groups, offer deeper insights into these aspects but may lack the rigor and generalizability of quantitative approaches. Artificial intelligence (AI) has the potential to revolutionize transport planning by providing more accurate predictions and optimizing decision-making processes, however, it requires that systems are transparent, accountable, and inclusive.

Ultimately, by combining these methods, planners and engineers can achieve a more comprehensive understanding of transport systems and develop solutions that are both evidence-based and context-sensitive—and this idea is at the core of this book, underscored by the concept of the Legitimacy, Accessibility, Social Learning, Transparency, and Representativeness (LASTR) framework. Using this mental model, Griffin lays out a systematic process for designing planning practices that are not only effective but also ethically sound. Griffin ties this construct to the principles of critical realism—with one of the central norms being recognizing the importance of sociotechnical systems.

Few books recognize the intricate link between transport and society; even fewer acknowledge how emerging transportation network technology further entwines these connections. Transportation systems encompass more than physical infrastructure—they include social practices, cultural norms, and political decisions. By adopting a sociotechnical lens, *Transport Truths* offers a roadmap for planners and policy makers to better understand how these elements interact and shape transportation policies and practices.

For instance, when planning a new transportation system, it is not enough to focus solely on technical aspects. Planners and engineers must also consider the social and cultural factors that influence its adoption and success. Engaging with stakeholders, understanding community needs, and designing systems that are accessible and equitable are all crucial components of this approach. This focus on inclusive transport planning processes is a core principle of the *Urban Transport Futures* series, and as such I could not be more excited about this volume.

Toward the end of my (2022) book, *End of the Road*, I referenced Pope Francis and his (2015) encyclical *Laudato si' On Care for Our Common Home*, saying: 'in an era where we face an unprecedented need to restore the environmental sanctity and social justice of our cities, I think it is important to consider how we take action ... and not separate environment and social challenges.'

Dr. Griffin's approach aligns with the same pragmatic and action-oriented approach, with the same respect for complex social and environmental crises our planet faces. *Transport Truths* espouses a radical empathy that can help us build a more livable world for us all. It offers a guidepost for better planning methods. And I believe it is an approach that will help planners, engineers and advocates uncover deeper meaning in the praxis of transport, and ultimately help us better care for our common home. Enjoy. Onward.

References

Pope Francis (2015) *Laudato si'*. Online May 24. Available from: http://w2.vatican.va/content/francesco/en/encyclicals/documents/papa-francesco_20150524_enciclica-laudato-si.html.

Riggs, W. (2022) *End of the Road: Reimagining the Street as the Heart of the City*, Bristol: Bristol University Press.

List of Figures, Tables, and Boxes

Figures

Tables

Boxes

Introduction: Methods and Ethics for Transport Analysis

On a warm June evening in San Antonio, Texas, Tina Galvan decided to take an e-scooter from one of the new shared schemes for a spin in the Government Hill residential district near downtown San Antonio. By the summer of 2019, e-scooter companies Bird, Lime, and Razor had rolled out systems rentable via smartphone apps, some of which required a brief safety guide before acceptance of their terms and conditions for use. Ms Galvan hit a small pothole and hit the asphalt hard.

'When I came to my knee was swollen so bad I couldn't walk and (it was) bleeding, my forehead was bleeding, my teeth had gone through my bottom lip and my arm was broken,' Ms Galvan told a radio reporter via telephone (Flahive, 2019). Galvan sued both Lime and the City of San Antonio for damages, claiming the scooter's design was not capable of safely navigating the pothole, which she could not see because of inadequate lighting and a lack of painted markings. Technologies—the new e-scooter, and the city's street conditions—were inadequate for the task, Galvan claimed.

E-scooter riders, the involved lawyers, and transport planners know that humans and technologies are intertwined factors in any transport problem. Industrial engineers designed the scooters with funding driven by venture capital, in a race to deliver the first, best product. City workers deliver services under political and economic conditions of their local council district, city, and sometimes regional, state, or federal funding. Everyday people traverse the city using complex ensembles of machines, navigation tools, and conversations with others about how to move around. One can reasonably expect that each actor in the transportation system that led to Ms Galvan's unfortunate crash could describe multiple versions of the story and evidence of the case to argue their perspective. It is possible that they might differ without one version necessarily being falsified by another. If described with ethical diligence, these various perspectives might all be true to some extent. Perhaps, they are all truths. Yet, one version might be more complete, more clear, more true, than the others. Understanding what really happens in transportation requires not only knowledge of the technologies and people involved, but how they create and redefine the events, mechanisms, and structures of transport systems as a sociotechnical ensemble.

Sociotechnical seeing for transport futures

If 'technology is society made durable' (Latour, 1990), then whether a technology supports ecological or human sustainability might be distinguished by tracing its development in the context of its application. The theoretical construct of sociotechnical systems can be a useful framework for transport planning because it recognizes that technology is not just a technical system, but it is also deeply embedded in social, cultural, and political systems.

Transportation systems are not just physical infrastructure, such as roads, bridges, and vehicles. They also involve social practices, cultural norms, and political decisions that influence how people move and interact in space. By using a sociotechnical lens in transport planning, planners can better understand the interactions between technology and social systems, and how these interactions shape the outcomes of transportation policies and practices.

For example, when planning a new transportation system, such as a new public transit line or bike-sharing program, planners can use a sociotechnical approach to consider not only the technical aspects of the system, but also the social and cultural factors that will impact its adoption and success. This may involve engaging with stakeholders, such as community members, to better understand their needs and preferences, and designing the system to be more accessible and equitable. These approaches address what is known as *procedural justice*—whether the transport planning process was fair across a community's population. Planning can also involve considering the broader political and economic factors that influence the adoption and success of transportation systems, such as funding, construction, and policies that regulate use and maintenance of the systems. These *distributive justice* factors impact who has access to jobs, family and friends, and resources (Pereira et al, 2017), which analysis can show how to improve through either equality in a single point in time, or by mitigating disadvantage, conscious of the impacts to disadvantaged groups over time. By thinking and working sociotechnically, planners can design more effective and sustainable transportation systems that better meet the needs of the communities they serve.

Transport planners, policy makers, students, and researchers may find this book valuable. Those interested in challenging the notion that a single story can or should guide transport policy and design decisions—whether told through everyday experiences, traditional engineering analyses, smart city sensors, or traffic forecasting models—will find resources and new ways of thinking about the problems. Hopefully, better thinking about transport problems will lead to more sustainable solutions for global futures. Students in planning, architecture, policy, and urban studies might find these approaches especially valuable, as they navigate rapid sociotechnical change that they will have to not only react to, but learn to address, with ethical frameworks that outlast technical and policy innovations and social appetite for implementing them.

Disciplines and disciples of transport planning

Planning, policy, and engineering disciplines produce knowledge in different ways, leading to misunderstandings and disbeliefs about how to produce equitable and just transport outcomes. Transport planning is concerned with the development and implementation of policies, strategies, and plans for the provision of transport services. The discipline typically draws on a range of data sources, including demographics, travel surveys, forecasting, and public engagement. They also consider broader issues, such as the impact of transport on the environment, social equity, and economic development.

Transport policy is concerned with the development and implementation of policies and regulations that govern the operation of transport systems. This discipline typically involves a range of stakeholders, including government agencies, transport operators, and advocacy groups. Transport policy can cover a wide range of issues, including safety, emissions, accessibility, and funding. Policy makers draw on research and analysis from a range of disciplines, including transport engineering, economics, and environmental science, to develop policy proposals.

Transport engineering is concerned with the design, construction, and operation of transport infrastructure and systems. This discipline typically involves the application of scientific and engineering principles to develop practical solutions to transport problems. Transport engineers use a range of tools and techniques, including traffic modeling, structural analysis, and systems integration, to design and evaluate transport infrastructure. They also work closely with other stakeholders, such as transport planners and policy makers, to ensure that transport solutions meet the needs of society.

Each of these disciplines has its own blind spots, which can cause problems in the transport development process. For example, transport planning may not always consider the practicalities of implementing transport options, such as the availability of funding or the feasibility of construction. Transport policy may not always consider the impact of regulations on the operation of transport systems, such as the effect of emissions standards on the cost of transport services. Transport engineering may not always consider the broader social, economic, and environmental impacts of transport infrastructure, such as the effect of road construction on local communities or the potential for air pollution from new transport systems.

This brief introduction to the different ways of seeing and sharing facts, opinions, observations, and perceptions across fields suggest that different ways of knowing impact how each approaches truth in practice. As an example, consider following a suburban dad's grocery shopping trip for a Saturday dinner. We will call him Marco. His nearest grocer that carries fresh vegetables is 2 km from home, on an arterial street on the edge of his neighborhood. We can directly observe his trip by following along behind in another car, but that would be time consuming to collect and difficult to manage, not to mention a bit creepy. So, we could use a pneumatic tube counter at the nearest collector street, which would record his crossing each direction as a puff of air as his tires compressed the rubber tube, completing a circuit in a board and recording the exact time of his trips. We could also ask him to complete a survey or record the trip on a smartphone app. These methods would provide much more information, but administering surveys can be very expensive. Marco's neighbors are recent immigrants working double shifts and raising two kids, so they declined to participate in the survey and are not included in the database. The regional transport planning agency aggregates all of the available data following well-established protocols, with graduate student interns following manuals to clean, anonymize, and aggregate the data into a database. Often, the interns have trip data that does not fit the protocol, or they misinterpret how the trip should be recorded—was his walking trip from a parking lot to the grocery store included in the trip? The intern asked a peer how they would code the trip, rather than bothering the supervisor. The database is marked as 'complete.' According to the transport agency's rules, the next plan several years later is created using Marco and others' aggregated trips into a computer model that can estimate travel volumes by time of day and road segment, approximating the overall travel as recorded in the database. The trip estimates are compared with the total number of trips counted several years ago, and then projected with the same factor of growth in traffic from the previous decade. According to agency policy, the growth factor assumes that Marco's teenagers will drive the same amount as he did, 20 years previously. The agency follows federal rules in order to remain competitive for new transport project funding—variations from the established forecasting methods require separate approvals and additional oversight and cost. Because the protocols were followed, the data and experts involved would be admissible as court evidence, if an environmental group were to sue the agency for local or global impacts. The actual impacts are largely impossible to observe, so lawsuits would largely ride on the opinions of experts, a judge, and perhaps a jury of citizens.

In this vignette, we gain a glimpse of how planners, engineers, policy makers, and others can use the same information about transport and not only arrive at different conclusions, but could plausibly estimate community impacts differently using the same original information. Observable events, such as Marco's trip to the grocery store, are obscured and adjusted, while his neighbor's trip was missed altogether. The mechanisms of transport planning follow protocols to attempt precision, but are actually nuanced social processes of learning and interpretation. A citizen juror might be surprised how much subjectivity—and policy guidance—undergirds an engineer's calculations. In this way, the truth of Marco's trip was never really known by anyone except Marco. Rather, each participant in the planning process builds their perception of reality through a socially filtered and constructed experience. Therefore, we see three levels of truths—an observation event of Marco's trip, the mechanisms of transport planning, and the legal and financial structures of the region and nation.

Mixed methods and the 'real world' of transport planning

Mixed methods, in the context of transport planning, denotes the integration of both qualitative and quantitative data. Mixed methods approaches seek to understand both the magnitude or breadth of an issue, while delving into questions about the how and why of an issue. This involves combining various strategies, methodologies, and data collection tools to create a comprehensive understanding of transportation systems. For instance, a Canadian team surveyed 281 bicyclists about their self-categorization of comfort with street bicycling, and then interviewed 25 of the same cyclists for insights on how the typology (mis)matched their lived experiences (Hosford et al, 2020). In a more practice-related study, Karen Lucas and team combined spatial analysis of large local datasets on a road bypass in Wales with participatory exercises with local residents, revealing ways that the project could be improved to minimize negative social impacts (Lucas et al, 2021). Mixed methods enables planners and policy makers to form a more nuanced understanding of transport realities by encompassing the complexity and diversity of user experiences, behaviors, and perspectives.

Planning is a discipline of mixed methods. Informed through my work as a professional planner in Texas over a decade before returning to academia, I found the 'real world' of transport planning often involves quantitative analysis of existing conditions in a community, review of public preferences, and a recommendation to policy makers, who are often democratically elected. These factors include human behavior, environmental concerns, policy regulations, technological advances, demographic changes, and economic conditions. Using mixed methods to navigate this complexity can offer more accurate, detailed, and context-specific insights. For instance, quantitative methods might involve statistical analysis of transport use, congestion patterns, or accident rates. These can provide a detailed overview of the current transport situation, but they may not capture the individual experiences and perceptions of users. On the other hand, qualitative methods could involve interviews or focus groups with public transport users, local residents, or transport employees. These can uncover people's attitudes towards transport services, their experiences with different modes of transport, and their reasons for their transport choices. When combined, these methods can complement each other and provide a holistic understanding of the transport situation. For example, the quantitative data might show a decline in bus use, while the qualitative data might reveal that this is due to perceptions of unreliability or inadequate service provision.

A failure to consider the full range of user experiences and perceptions can lead to the marginalization of certain groups or the overlooking of critical safety issues. Therefore, employing mixed methods in transport planning can contribute to more ethical, equitable, and effective transport solutions. However, practitioners make choices in how they work based in part on the practices of their disciplines.

The nexus of methods and ethics in transport practice

Choosing a method to address a transport question has ethical implications. Choosing a method to address a research question in transportation research not only determines the type of data collected and conclusions drawn but can also have significant ethical implications. The research methods chosen directly influence the inclusion or exclusion of specific population groups, the type of data used for decision-making, and the balance of power in policy making.

Suppose a researcher chooses to use a quantitative method, such as a large-scale survey or statistical analysis of transportation usage data. While this method might provide valuable data on overall patterns and trends, it may fail to capture the full complexity of individual experiences, especially those of marginalized or underrepresented groups.

For instance, a quantitative study might reveal that few people use a particular bus route, leading decision-makers to consider eliminating it. However, qualitative research, such as interviews or focus groups, might reveal that this route is crucial for a specific population group, like the elderly or those without access to private transportation. Overreliance on quantitative data might thus lead to decisions that are disadvantageous or even harmful to marginalized populations, raising ethical concerns about social justice and equity.

Another ethical implication in method choice arises in the balance of power between transport users and experts. If researchers primarily rely on expert analysis, such as engineers' assessments of road quality, they may neglect the experiences and insights of those who actually use the transport system.

On the contrary, incorporating user feedback, for example, through public consultations or participatory mapping, can provide a different perspective and democratize the decision-making process. Failure to do so can lead to decisions that are disconnected from user needs and experiences, raising ethical issues about democratic representation and the right to the city.

In conclusion, the choice of research methods in transportation studies can have profound ethical implications. Therefore, researchers should strive for a balanced approach, combining different methods to achieve a comprehensive, inclusive, and equitable understanding of transportation realities.

From each discipline's perspective, methods and ethics align. But other disciplines may consider a method inappropriate, or unethical. The disciplines of urban planning, civil engineering, and public administration each bring unique perspectives to transportation research, often defining appropriate methods based on their distinct orientations and priorities. This results in a diverse range of approaches to understanding and addressing transportation issues, but it can also lead to varying ethical implications.

Urban planners typically focus on how transportation systems affect and integrate with broader urban systems. They often use a variety of methods, including spatial analysis, land use planning, public consultation, and policy analysis. Urban planners are particularly concerned with how transport decisions affect social equity, environmental sustainability, and urban livability. A key ethical issue here can arise when the views and needs of certain population groups, especially marginalized communities, are not adequately incorporated into planning processes or outcomes, leading to disparities in access to transportation.

Civil engineers often emphasize technical and quantitative methods, including traffic modeling, safety analysis, and infrastructure design. Their primary concerns often revolve around efficiency, safety, and the technical feasibility of transport systems. One potential ethical issue in this discipline can stem from an overemphasis on technical solutions at the expense of social or environmental considerations. For instance, focusing on car-centric infrastructure may lead to unintended consequences such as urban sprawl, environmental degradation, and the marginalization of non-motorized transport users.

Public administration, in the context of transportation, often involves policy development, financial management, and organizational governance. Methods here might include policy analysis, cost-benefit analysis, stakeholder consultation, and organizational review. Ethical issues in public administration can emerge when there is a lack of transparency in decision-making, conflicts of interest, or inequitable distribution of resources. For instance, a lack of public participation in decision-making processes can lead to policies that do not adequately reflect public needs or preferences.

In summary, each discipline brings essential insights to transportation research but can also introduce unique ethical challenges. Re-considering how we use knowledge across disciplines could foster a more holistic approach to transport planning that coordinates each discipline's approach.

The use and misuse of knowledge for transport planning

Transport planning involves understanding flows of people and goods across space and time. At its simplest, data on these flows in a geographic area, categorized by travel mode, provides the basis upon which planners can make knowledgeable decisions about investments needed to achieve a desired future. However, the data is never complete or comprehensive for all past times, which is only one of the challenges complicating estimating future conditions. Traffic forecasts are the least accurate form of information in transport planning, while they may also be the most important.

Transport planners can get more than the future wrong. Many of the decisions in what information to gather for a planning project may be guided by political decisions of agency heads. Hired consultants may lean towards what they think the heads of a hiring agency would want them to analyze, regardless of whether the project scope defines that information. But political pressures are not the only reasons planners mis-diagnose or prescribe faulty solutions. As humans, they bring individual experiences and preferences—they might favor preferences of certain community groups, or prefer avoiding working with the public altogether. Every opportunity to make a right decision is also one they could get wrong.

Error and bias are a persistent problem, with documented research on the issues spanning generational timescales (Mackie and Preston, 1998). Mackie and Preston identified 21 separate forms of bias and error, ranging from 'unclear objectives or conflicts between stated and actual objectives' to 'appraisal optimism'—which the authors find 12 of their listed problems recursively feed into. Any form of data, including those with errors and biases, get multiplied when modeled into future conditions required in planning.

Measurement biases can include all of the variances between how a sensor collects data and actual movements in space. Linnet Taylor described how mobility data from phones can mis-represent individual travel by assuming that one phone SIM card is used by one person. People may use multiple SIM cards to access different cell networks in different locations, or an entire family may share one phone (Taylor, 2016). Measurement bias could include many other problems with sensors: batteries dying, GPS satellite configurations reducing accuracy, maintenance issues, and more. Transport planners cannot typically solve these problems upstream of their data sources, but expert interviewees suggested planners can perform analyses to filter out unreasonable data points (Griffin et al, 2020).

Sometimes, building a new road may make traffic worse. Originally described in 1968 by a German mathematician, Braess's Paradox is a counter-intuitive phenomenon observed in transportation networks and other systems where the addition of resources or infrastructure, such as roads or highways, can actually lead to worsened overall performance (Braess et al, 2005). The paradox occurs when adding a new road to the network results in longer travel times for everyone, rather than the shorter travel times you might expect. When a new road is added, some drivers will switch to what they perceive as a quicker route. This can lead to overutilization of the new road and underutilization of the old ones. The additional congestion can result in longer travel times for all drivers, even those who did not change their route. This paradox is related to the more commonly-known phenomenon of induced demand—building new, unpriced travel lanes increases the demand for the product, yielding more and more traffic (Fields and Renne, 2021). However, empirical studies suggest that the paradox that is plainly visible in small modeling networks might be difficult to detect in most real functioning networks (Levinson et al, 2017). Smartphone navigation apps can help users find optimal paths that balance traffic on a network (Bittihn and Schadschneider, 2021). Mitigating Braess's Paradox in transportation planning involves understanding and considering the larger system dynamics when designing and adjusting networks. Critical analysis of the traffic forecasting process that considers induced demand—from in-between project staff members, and public critique through involvement with decisionmakers—can help prevent planning of networks that ironically worsen traffic through Braess's Paradox.

Demographic biases in transportation planning can create a vicious cycle of under-representation leading to disinvestment through planning decisions. Males are over-represented in the planning, engineering, and elected leadership roles in the United States and many other countries, leading to unbalanced transportation planning decisions. Under-represented people in transportation planning span dimensions of race, gender, ethnicity, and intersectionality. A lack of deep understanding from the community's perspective, known in Weberian sociology as *verstehen*—is the result of under-representation of these groups in transport planning. Tara Goddard and colleagues' surveys in northern California showed that 'men report that they drive significantly more miles than women, and among workers, women stop on the way home significantly more often than men. Men also tend to work more days per week and have longer temporal and spatial commutes' (Goddard et al, 2006, p 143). Their finding supports other work showing a clear priority of peak-traffic work commuting in transportation planning, leading to investments that support longer-distance travel—which may exacerbate urban sprawl (Handy, 2005). Gender bias in developing countries can be worse, due to reduced access to travel modes and technologies. Even when technologies like bicycles or cars are available, women in developing countries may have less purchasing power, or experience social discrimination that discourages their use (Rosenbloom and Pleissis-Fraissard, 2010). Globally, harassment and safety concerns further discourage women from walking, biking, or riding transit in certain situations, exacerbating challenges for equitable and sustainable travel. Gender is only one dimension of bias—people of color, lower-income groups, marginalized social communities, and especially people living at the intersections of multiple under-represented communities experience disproportional outcomes from transportation planning. These studies suggest that gender and other biases of under-representation need to be addressed both in planning, and then in post-implementation outcomes, to improve transportation equity. Under-representation is the more systematic problem, however. Hiring women and under-represented groups in planning and engineering roles, and voting them into leadership positions, are the long-term solutions.

Road networks are planned differently over time, and tend to stay in place for a very long time. Researchers studying how much of a network is built into a grid of four-road intersections, or how roads are built at different angles versus aligned together, can help reveal changes in how human settlements deal with road congestion and pollution. However, Burghardt et al (2022) showed that trends of these characteristics across the US fall apart when analyzed at regional or city-level geographies. This breakdown of understanding is called Simpson's paradox—an inference in overall trends can reverse when analyzing sub-categories of the same dataset (Simpson, 1951). To prevent misinterpretations, analysts can draw simple diagrams of expected causal relationships based on previous knowledge. These causal diagrams can help clarify assumptions and reveal factors that could mediate or reverse relationships in transport planning. Witmer (2021) shows approaches to diagram relationships and graph data to solve whether aggregated data or conditional analysis are needed—how we can avoid being blinded by Simpson's paradox.

Despite these well-documented challenges for understanding the present and future transport conditions, planners and researchers can take some big-picture steps to control the impacts of bias and paradoxes in their analyses. Mackie and Preston suggest 'three antidotes' (1998, p 6). The first is for transport agencies to build internal teams with a specific function to evaluate transport assessments, rather than the projects themselves. Next, they call for open scrutiny of proposed projects by the public, with 'adequate resources to cross-examine the scheme promoters.' Finally, they recommend devoting much more time and resources to ex post evaluation of projects, to evaluate forecasts against reality. With the exception of Flyvbjerg (1998) and a few others, few post-project appraisals fully engage with the realities of what options planners

Table 1.1: Sampling of biases and paradoxes in planning

Bias or paradox	Realm of transport	Why	How to address
Braess's Paradox	Traffic network planning	Road network expansions may redistribute traffic, increasing travel time	• Critical analysis of traffic forecasting that considers induced demand
Demographic bias	Problem definition	Gender-blind planning can lead to investments that more often support male travel patterns	• Gender-sensitive planning • Evaluation of post-implementation project outcomes
Optimism bias	Traffic forecasting	Studies omit factors that dampen infrastructure use	• External review of forecasts • Reference class forecasting
Measurement bias	Data collection	Any sensor problem can produce data that misleads planners	• Analysis and filtering of incorrect data
Aggregation bias	Data analysis	Big data is grouped for privacy and efficiency, obscuring travel resolution	• Some modeling techniques can re-estimate data in space or time
Simpson's Paradox	Causal inference of transportation decisions	Overall trends may reverse in sub-categories	• Causal diagramming • Sub-category analysis

truly have to shape project processes and results. As Flyvbjerg states, 'power has a rationality that power does not know' (Flyvbjerg, 1998, p 225).

Table 1.1, sampling of biases and paradoxes in planning, can be helpful to guide research design and improve the accuracy of answers to the posited research questions. But how do we determine if the *question* itself is valuable? Based on an extensive review of previous studies of transport planning, technological changes, and an acknowledgement that reality may not be fully observable, I propose five dimensions of analysis to seek transport truths: legitimacy, accessibility, social learning, transparency, and representativeness (Griffin, 2019).

The Legitimacy, Accessibility, Social Learning, Transparency, and Representativeness (LASTR) framework for planning truths

Readers concerned with the process and results of transport planning see that how we know what we think we know is not always clear. The LASTR framework provides a way to delve into wicked, sociotechnical planning cases by separating critical topics and depth of analysis. This section provides a very brief introduction to the approach explained further in my work at The University of Texas at Austin (Griffin, 2019), and then connects that approach to a philosophy of science called critical realism. A critical realist perspective on transport planning expects that phenomena like transport (dis)investments have impacts on society that exist whether they have been uncovered or described. Roy Baskar, one of the progenitors of this philosophy, suggests that critical realism helps understand the connections between observable events (such as a construction proposal) from the structures that underlie those events (including the socio-political expectations of project funding and re-election of political leaders). Baskar suggests that 'we will only be able to understand—and so change—the social world if we identify the structures at work that generate those events or discourses. Such structures are irreducible to the patterns of events and discourses alike. These structures are not spontaneously apparent in the observable pattern of events; they can only be identified through the practical and theoretical work of the social sciences' (Bhaskar, 2010, p 2). Examples from recent scholarship help describe why and how the LASTR framework can help distinguish reality to improve transport planning through social science. Through this perspective, we can find that identifying truths allow more productive work to address the problems of equity that transport changes can unleash in our communities.

Legitimacy of a planning process is the degree to which the process is designed to effect real outcomes. Previous studies found legitimacy is supported by early-stage process deliberation between planners and politicians (Legacy, 2010), and harmed when engagement is designed to broadly appear genuine but lacking substance (Thorpe, 2017). Sherry Arnstein's Ladder of Citizen Participation and John Forester's enabling rules and organizing practices (Arnstein, 1969; Forester, 1980) set the stage for an understanding of how to understand legitimacy in planning, albeit in different ways. Legitimacy has an increasing role in each of the rungs on Arstein's ladder, which I italicize in this section for clarity. Arnstein uses examples of community action agencies to show how the 'bodies frequently have no legitimate function or power,' but are used to cause the appearance of real involvement—only serving as a form of *manipulation* (Arnstein, 1969, p 218). She describes a tweak of manipulative approaches to promote intra-group communication as a form of *therapy*. *Informing* turns this approach around to information flow from a planning agency to the public, but notes that 'informing citizens of their rights, responsibilities, and options can be the most important first step toward legitimate citizen participation' (Arnstein, 1969, p 219). The fourth rung is *consultation*, noting that at least 'inviting citizens' opinions, like informing them, can be a legitimate step toward their full participation' (Arnstein, 1969, p 219). In *placation, planners* 'allow citizens to advise or plan ad infinitum but retain for powerholders the right to judge the legitimacy or feasibility of the advice' (Arnstein, 1969, p 220). *Partnership* and *delegated power* represent higher levels of citizen control, where legitimacy is apparent through cooperative action. *Citizen control* is the final rung, involving full decision-making authority by publics, with planning staff and officials in a support role. Most recent research on public engagement uses the Arnstein Ladder as a conceptual metaphor, rather than developing rigorous performance measures aligned with rungs. Forester's pragmatic communication expects others to speak comprehensively (relating to all pertinent issues), sincerely (following actual intentions), legitimately (aligning pertinent facts and perspectives), and truthfully (avoiding falsehoods) (Forester, 1980). Forester describes that we experience distortions of legitimacy in planning through face-to-face communication when issues can be described out of context; organizationally when staff are unresponsive or dominant; and regarding a political-economic structure when an agency is not accountable for actions. Each of these can also apply to online communication through communication between individuals (one-to-one), organizations and individuals (many-to-one), and in the structures of economic and political feedback between publics and planning agencies. In a democratic society, a planning process that is legitimate must also be available to the public.

Accessibility involves the ability of members of the public to involve themselves in a planning process. Accessibility involves spatial, temporal, and availability of the process from the perspective of language and technical skills. Online participation methods offer significant advantages regarding spatial and temporal access, but are limited by language and technical availability—termed the digital divide (Sui et al, 2013). Nonetheless, online methods show significant prospect regarding the number of participants. A recent study of online and face-to-face participation in Poland showed an increase of five (geo-discussion) and 40 times (geo-questionnaire) the number of participants attending in-person meetings (Jankowski et al, 2016). This recent example also included similar levels of participation between different levels of education—showing that online or in-person participation do not necessarily bias participation among those with higher education. However, online participants were on average 7 years younger, suggesting a role to continue both techniques to support diverse ages of participants. This is consistent with online access polls in the United States, with the digital divide lessening by income, education, and race, but with persistent lag for older persons (Pew Research Center, 2016). Making processes available says little about impacts to those who participate—they should gain real knowledge from their engagement.

Social learning in planning involves gaining or sharing knowledge or skills between participants in a planning process—including staff and publics.

The idea of learning as both a precursor and positive side effect of civic participation is a tradition in pragmatic notions of democracy. Previous studies suggest that social learning in planning requires communicative and informatics components—that social learning 'depends on the transfer or flow of information' (Gudowsky and Bechtold, 2013, p 7) that can be supported by technological tools in social contexts (Stewart et al, 2018). Taking a broader perspective, John Dewey suggests that a good idea can spread, even beginning with a single participant:

> The important consideration is that opportunity be given [for] that idea to spread and to become the possession of the multitude. No government by experts in which the masses do not have the chance to inform the experts as to their needs can be anything but an oligarchy managed in the interests of the few. And the enlightenment must proceed in ways which force the administrative specialists to take account of the needs. (Dewey, 1927, p 208)

Dewey did not describe *how* ideas spread, however, which were later articulated through the ideas of communicative action (Habermas, 1990), network society (Castells, 2007), and social capital (Wilson, 1997). A primary condition of knowledge sharing and developing networks is the level of openness for participation—which is one way to see the characteristic of transparency.

Transparency has to do with the ability of people outside an organizational process to be able to find and answer questions about how decisions are made. In this way, transparency is intermingled with the concept of accountability—visible and coherent information about a process that helps ensure government decisions align with public needs (Pak et al, 2017). Participants consider transparency as a requirement for trusting a planning organization, a key component of cultural capital for public planning (Mandarano, 2015). In planning processes, we can think of transparency both in terms of the degree that participants can find and understand the process of planning, in addition to the data and information used in that process. Transparent planning processes lend themselves to clear evaluation by people outside the process (Laurian et al, 2010). Government officials may see this as both an advantage and disadvantage, where increasing transparency may also expose problems that staff need to solve or help people see where and why their participation is not used in decision making. Transparency is not a binary decision for planning organizations—it is gradational and multi-dimensional, in addition to being inherently uneven. Transparency takes leadership in organizations—including public, non-governmental, and community-based.

Representation in planning processes can be understood as both how the public's views guide decision-making, but also the ways that data or information characterizes the phenomena of interest. Differences in digital access can translate into discrepancies of 'computer and internet abilities,' known as *techno-capital*, deepening inequities of access to opportunities (McConnell, 2014). Though the disparity of internet access between these groups has dropped over time, online participation alone will not reach significant portions of the population—the same demographics likely to be at risk from planning outcomes like displacement in the first place (Sandoval, 2007). Big data approaches to representing transportation behavior or planning preferences pose risks as well. Interviews with experts in transportation big data show that these new approaches track devices rather than people, likely biasing those most able to purchase the items or spend money on toll transactions and other easily-tracked behaviors (Griffin et al, 2020). Representation biases in participation create a quandary for planners—if participants do not reflect the population, empowering the *participating* public could further marginalize those that could not participate.

By separating these five components of planning processes and outcomes, LASTR enables comparison of complex cases against each other, and offers some standardization to help define 'good' planning. Integrating the components across planning cases allows researchers and practitioners a repeatable approach to project evaluation that could be implemented for only an ongoing process as will be done in this book's two cases, or for evaluating outcomes after completion. Regardless, this book will argue for integrating a mixed methods approach using a critical realist framework.

Given this introduction to some of the challenges with evaluating complex transport planning cases, and some of the approaches to thinking and working through them, it is time for a review of what this chapter has offered.

Contributions

This introductory chapter laid a groundwork for why typical approaches to transport practice and research provide glimpses of reality, but a more comprehensive analysis approach is needed. Recognizing that planning practice almost always includes some sort of rational or empirical analysis, followed by a more qualitative review from agency leaders, elected officials, and hopefully the publics affected by the decisions, it is only reasonable that research works to retain similar breadth with rigor.

To understand transport planning, this chapter has argued that we have to expand the ways we think and work with cases in a more comprehensive manner, even if we have to recognize limits of time and resources to perform the work. Regardless of discipline, this chapter argues for considering four approaches to understanding transport truths, which form the basis for how this book approaches transport case studies.

Sociotechnical seeing recognizes that technology does not 'cause' changes in society by sheer force of engineering innovation. Rather, technologies are enmeshed with social processes from the origin of an idea, through research and development, prototyping, and eventual implementation. Economic and social conditions, local cultures, and global social conditions are the main drivers of technology adoption, which includes new transport modes, infrastructures, and the interfaces people use to access transport systems. Since the social cannot be divorced from the technical, this book advocates for attention to more than one approach to understanding the wicked problems of transportation.

Mixed methods and critical realism provide ways of knowing and being that align with a complicated and integrated approach. A critical realist perspective on transport expects that people's engagement with transport has actual impacts at local and global scales over time, but that only some of these factors may be fundamentally knowable. We can observe transport events by counting traffic, asking participants about impacts on their lives, and gain understanding of the mechanisms by which people and transport systems interact, conflict, and deliver goods and services across economies and cultures. In doing so, some of the underlying structures that cause positive or negative changes in these interactions may be observed—if only a glimpse of the complicated realities. This way of understanding transport is not limited to academic studies, but can guide practical transport analysis by practitioners. This kind of approach to transport practice enables a broader and deeper understanding of transport truths, while valuing the multitude of perspectives that planners find by interacting with local communities, expert practitioners, and elected officials. The challenge of knowing more about transport systems is how to integrate more that we know about reality with our notions of what good planning should achieve.

Aligning methods and ethics explicitly allows transport analysts to openly confront the fact that there is no such thing as unbiased analysis. Since everyone has a background of experiences, values, disciplinary perspectives, and vision, open consideration of how these inform how we perform transport planning can lead to more truthful engagement personally, and in how our projects impact communities over time. Practitioners and researchers should engage with our backgrounds and the known biases common to transport listed in this chapter to seriously confront the friction between what we expect is good, against how our disciplines, communities, and even laws guide our work. The LASTR framework helps break down components of how we can evaluate good transport planning processes and outcomes, integrated with our ways of knowing.

When Tina Galvan had that e-scooter crash one evening in San Antonio, she was probably just looking for a fun way to get around, rather than helping demonstrate the observability of individual transport events, and the relative obscurity of underlying causal mechanisms and socio-technical-political structures. Nonetheless, the intertwined technological innovation, policies, laws, and social practices that led to her mishap could be traced through the lenses of legitimacy, accessibility, social learning, transparency, and representativeness. The next chapter explains why the transport disciplines have struggled to build a comprehensive approach to transport analysis and planning, along with how to integrate this approach with a critical realist perspective.

Box 1.1: Introductory takeaways for practice

- Transport planners address problems with qualitative and quantitative information, balancing observations, biases and ethics.
- Recognizing that technologies and societies are intertwined prevents false assumptions of innovations causing changes separately from culture and human communication.
- Seeking a 'good' planning process and outcomes involves legitimacy, accessibility, social learning, transparency, and representativeness.

2

A Biased History
of Transport Futures

Every description of a transport context in the past or present is incomplete. There are always human experiences that remain unknown, just as with nonhuman impacts, such as to biota or structures. Conceiving futures about transport systems are even more fraught. Forecasting models rely on past data that was qualitatively chosen and manipulated, just as narratives we can tell about the future are fueled by personal experiences. Each perspective—each truth—is biased.

We must engage with the reality that any description of transport phenomena requires qualitative choices that guide which versions of data and stories the researcher or practitioner deems most important. To do so requires a critical review of how the way we think about these issues informs how we grasp reality, choosing between transport truths to guide decision-making. The thought process changes as an individual experiences, recalls, and selectively forgets knowledge about transport contexts. This experiential knowledge only scales up to organizational change to the extent that the experiences are communicated, recorded, and encoded as organizational changes.

This chapter shows four evolutions in how transport planners think: economic rationality, mobility vs. access, the role of public input, and dashboarding information for transport planning. Additionally, this chapter shows how each of these topics intersect with the LASTR framework—legitimacy, accessibility, social learning, transparency, and representativeness all play a role in transport planning's effectiveness, and can be analyzed in cases through a critical realist perspective.

Economic man and the myth of pragmatism

Transport planning as applied in modeling relies on economic theories, including the mythical or limited applicability of 'economic man' who makes decisions based solely on time and costs, with no consideration of altruism, fun, or other humanistic approaches. The 'economic man' or 'homo economicus' theory is an economic concept that assumes individuals always act rationally and in their self-interests, with full access to information, aiming to maximize utility in each decision. This theory underlies many economic models and has been used in urban transport planning, for instance, to model how individuals might choose between different modes of transport based on cost and time factors. However, the 'economic man' theory is a simplification and falls short in several key respects. First, it assumes that individuals have perfect knowledge of their options, which is often not the case in the real world. Second, it assumes that individuals only consider economic factors when making decisions, ignoring the reality that decisions are also influenced by social, cultural, and personal factors. For example, an individual might choose to cycle rather than drive for health or environmental reasons (Griffin and Jiao, 2015b; Frank et al, 2019), even if bicycling may be less time efficient. Third, it assumes a level of individualism and autonomy that may not be applicable in all cases—for instance, a parent might need to consider their children's school schedules when planning their commute.

Pragmatism, on the other hand, emphasizes practicality and rejects the notion that there is a single, universal truth. As a philosophy, John Dewey and others argued that pragmatism values experience and inquiry (Morgan, 2014), which intuitively fits the needs of planners working towards big visions within the constraints of democratic governments. Planning scholars have re-invigorated pragmatic philosophy for social progress, while recognizing its limitations. Tore Sager revisited John Forester's critical communicative pragmatism, suggesting that the communicative approach imposes political costs through its requirements for managing power relationships, limiting communicative pragmatism as a practical approach for planners (Sager, 2006). Similarly, William Lester argues that planning's recent communicative paradigm can restrict bold visionary approaches, while the pragmatic approach of 'redescription' can help reduce these challenges. He sees this approach as guiding planners toward seeking social progress, rather than truth (Lester, 2022). Primarily, its focus on the practical can lead to short-termism and a disregard for broader theoretical insights, which can be valuable for understanding the underlying dynamics of transport systems. Additionally, while context-specific solutions are important, a purely pragmatic approach may overlook the potential benefits of universal principles or standards, which can provide a useful foundation for transport planning. In the context of urban transport, this might mean focusing on what works in specific contexts and disregarding overarching theories. This approach is valuable in its recognition of the complex, multifaceted nature of urban transport, and it can encourage innovative, context-specific solutions. Overall, pragmatism may disregard the impact of power dynamics and structural inequalities on transport systems, potentially leading to solutions that serve the interests of the powerful at the expense of marginalized groups. Perhaps truth has more value for urban planning than pragmatic philosophy can support.

While both the 'economic man' theory and pragmatic philosophy provide useful perspectives on urban transport, neither offers a comprehensive understanding of this complex system. A holistic approach to urban transport planning needs to consider the full range of economic, social, cultural, and political factors at play, and must be mindful of both the specificities of local context and the insights offered by broader theoretical frameworks. Much of the transport system in the US was developed with a pragmatic, economic-oriented mindset that led to emphasizing mobility. These approaches can be evaluated through a lens of legitimacy—pragmatic approaches can work in real practice. However, work on social justice shows that equitable plans are not the same as equitable outcomes. One truth is undeniably simple: planners should address transport from the perspective of getting people where they need to go.

Access as a paradigm incorporating location

While mobility is a straightforward goal to aim for—the ability to move freely—it does not necessarily get people where they want to go. Since the middle of the previous century, departments of transportation—particularly in the US—have focused on providing mobility by building a hierarchical street network that focuses on speed. Despite the intuitive problem of focusing on mobility rather than access, change has been slow. However, transport research has further demonstrated the concept of access, affecting federal transport policies. Changing the professional paradigm towards access—the ability to reach destinations—requires thinking about land use and transport at the same time (Levine et al, 2019).

Research on transport access shows its importance for 21st-century grand challenges, including social equity, environmental stewardship, and mitigating human-caused climate change. Globally, access to jobs increases with population density, but sprawling land use in US cities is a main factor in unequal access to jobs by travel mode. Access to jobs by walking in European cities is comparable to Nairobi or Douala in Africa, while US cities have the lowest access to jobs by walking (Wu et al, 2021). Accessibility is also related to quality of life. A study of Colorado (US) residents reported that 'having more transportation choices can improve standard of living for low- and middle-income residents' (Makarewicz and Németh, 2017, p 179). The global trends also play out in detailed analysis of the San Francisco Bay Area. Golub and Martens performed an empirical analysis with a social justice perspective, showing that access to jobs by car versus public transit varies almost all areas of the region, creating areas of 'access poverty' (Golub and

Martens, 2014, p 10). Their mapping shows the inequitable access in a region not just to highlight problems—doing so gives planners clear ways to plan projects that could improve access equity. Planning emphasizing mobility can also have environmental impacts, due in part by induced travel. Beyond the direct impacts of building new or expanded highways, the additional mobility—often measured as Vehicle Kilometers Traveled (VKT)—are often ignored in environmental assessments (Noland, 2007). David Banister integrated previous studies on sustainable transportation, showing the links between cities, mobility, and climate change (Banister, 2011). He argues that 'sustainable mobility provides a new paradigm within which to investigate the complexity of cities, and to strengthen the links between land use and transport,' including the shift from planning for mobility to accessibility, to reduce the need for travel, make it easier to use a variety of travel modes, and to reduce the distances needed for trips (Banister, 2011, p 1540). Emphasizing access over mobility is a key concept in the sustainable mobility paradigm, which has impacted policy making and transport investments for more than a decade. What is less clear is how new data-rich methods are changing how planners, agency officials, and publics perceive needs for transport system changes.

Use of the term access in the transport sense is not fully separate from accessibility to planning information. Perhaps access to information can help guide sustainable transitions.

Dashboards for decisions?

Concepts like access to jobs, environmental indicators, social equity measures, and similar are usually quantifiable, critical for impactful planning, and complicated. Dashboards, usually implemented as clear graphs or dynamic infographics showing current measures and trends, can convey these critical measures for broad audiences, including on simple web pages. The City of London launched the City Datastore in 2010, powering a CityDashboard with visualizations of traffic and bikeshare usage (Gray et al, 2016). Companies who compile urban data also create dashboards, which may be intended to demonstrate their products as much as providing direct insights. Ride Report has developed a dashboard of micromobility, integrating their city clients' information and clarifying key metrics for this emerging set of transportation modes, spanning cities in Australia, New Zealand, and the US (Ride Report, 2023). The Micromobility Dashboard shows an aggregated 'Global Micromobility Index' of trends over time, in addition to allowing users to drill into individual cities, and even download trip data aggregated to avoid sharing personally-identifiable information. City subscribers gain information about emerging modes in their cities, in addition to making a publicly-available dashboard. At their best, urban dashboards can make information more publicly accessible and current, with real-time data provided by urban sensors and media, potentially improving decision-making.

However, scholars across urban arts and sciences show challenges for using urban dashboards to guide decisions. Some see the approach as more than just a convenient and clear approach to understanding urban challenges. Rather, they argue that the dashboard changes the way we know a city—a new urban epistemology. Rob Kitchen and colleagues showed how these changes come to light, viewing 'the city as visualised facts—that is reshaping how managers and citizens come to know and govern cities' (Kitchin et al, 2015, p 6). After recognizing the potential benefits, they find dashboards to be 'underpinned by a naive instrumental rationality, are open to manipulation by vested interests, and suffer from often unacknowledged methodological and technical issues' (Kitchin et al, 2015, p 6). In an historical review of dashboards starting with NASA's Mission Control to recent cities' efforts to clarify data-driven administration, Shannon Mattern problematizes the approach as a solution to urban problems (Mattern, 2015). The dashboards' simplicity is also its limitation, by over-simplification of reality, she argues. Deciding which measures to include on a dashboard imposes importance on the subject, implying that other measures matter less, if at all. Because they do not contextualize the information, people can mistake aesthetics or clarity from understanding. 'If the city is understood as the sum of its component widgets, residents have an impoverished sense of how they can act as urban subjects' (Mattern, 2015). Rather than reflecting the cities that dashboards are meant to convey, dashboard design and visualization has an active role in framing and managing the city. Arguments for and against urban dashboards nonetheless demonstrate that deciding which quantitative measure to highlight is a qualitative choice—each city is an assemblage of multiple truths.

All of these scholars provide insight on the opportunities and limits of dashboards for transport and other urban challenges. Yet, social learning is at the root of what is missing from these arguments. The degree to which dashboards can foster communities and experts learning together—by communicating new perspectives on transport information—might be a more useful approach. If dashboards over-simplify urban problems, perhaps more data could lead to richer understanding and different decisions.

Public input from civil rights to crowdsourcing

Transport planning has been significantly shaped by societal transformations and technological innovations over the years. Particularly, the evolution of public input in transport planning, from the civil rights era to the modern age of crowdsourcing, demonstrates this shift vividly.

During the civil rights era in the US, the public's role in transport planning was mainly reactive, constrained by limited channels of communication and socio-political circumstances. The racial segregation, rampant inequality, and discriminatory practices in urban planning of this period often limited the efficacy of public participation, confining it to protests, boycotts, and court cases, such as the Montgomery Bus Boycott, spurred by the arrest of Rosa Parks, who refused to ride in the back of the racially-segregated bus. Title VI of the Civil Rights Act of 1964 prohibited discrimination in programs receiving financial assistance from the federal government and required community participation plans (US Department of Transportation, 2022b). These plans required meaningful public engagement with those who would be impacted by the projects and served as a template for later state and local requirements. These actions reflected dissatisfaction and initiated incremental changes, yet they were not characterized by consistent, proactive public input in planning processes.

Post-war growth in roadway funding at federal, then state and local levels, led to a construction boom that spurred urban sprawl, much of which happened with little coordination between governments and publics.

> In late 1969 the basic guidelines for the 3C [continuous, comprehensive, and cooperative] planning process were amended to require citizen participation in all phases of the planning process from the setting of goals through the analysis of alternatives. Consequently, it became the responsibility of the planning agency to seek out public views. (Weiner, 1997, p 70)

Additionally, the idea of public input as a necessary element of transport planning was solidified further by landmark legislations like the National Environmental Policy Act of 1969, which required comprehensive environmental reviews including public hearings. The US Federal-Aid Highway Act of 1973, however, marked a significant turning point. The Act funded planning work through metropolitan planning organizations (MPOs), regional bodies charged with overseeing transportation planning that were mandated to involve the public (Weiner, 1997). Through the Intermodal Surface Transportation Efficiency Act of 1991 (ISTEA), MPOs had to formalize their public engagement processes in the process of developing long-range transportation plans and the transportation improvement programs that solidified funding for individual projects.

The advent of digital technologies, however, has revolutionized the way public input is solicited, aggregated, and utilized in transport planning. In particular, internet and social media have democratized information, allowing for increased transparency and public participation, in addition to providing a platform for misinformation and discord. Nevertheless, the information asymmetry that once existed between planners and the public has significantly diminished.

With the arrival of the 21st century, crowdsourcing has emerged as a pioneering tool for garnering public input. Crowdsourcing refers to the practice of obtaining information, ideas, or services by soliciting contributions to an organization from a large group of people, primarily online (Brabham, 2013). Platforms like Waze and Strava collect real-time transport data from users to optimize routes, and can help provide an evidence base for transport performance measures and studies. In the realm of planning, crowdsourcing provides a powerful means of participatory planning by enabling direct, widespread public input. Platforms like StreetMix allow citizens to design their own street layouts, while apps like Commonplace solicit community opinions on local development proposals. In addition, interactive online mapping tools and surveys have become popular means of gathering public preferences on transportation plans. Through crowdsourcing, planners can tap into a larger pool of perspectives, ostensibly to foster a more inclusive planning process. To test how public input technologies differ by geographic availability and extensive use for bicycle planning, I led a study of in-person meetings, an interactive online map, and a smartphone application that tracked bicycle routes and ratings (Griffin, 2019), finding that 'both online techniques resulted in a larger geography for participation than in-person meetings, with the regional PPGIS [public participation geographic information system] covering the most area' (Griffin and Jiao, 2019b, p 460). However, there could be cases that show more the opposite. Regardless, multiple public outreach methods are more likely to improve most engagement outcomes. Technologies for participatory planning can mitigate the limitations of traditional public meetings, which are often attended by a small, unrepresentative sample of the population. Importantly, it also empowers communities to articulate their own visions for transportation, moving beyond reaction to proactive engagement and social learning.

The evolution of public input in transport planning reflects broader societal and technological changes. From the reactive participation of the civil rights era, public input has shifted towards proactive engagement, aided by the democratizing forces of digital technology and crowdsourcing. As we move further into the digital age, these tools promise even more sophisticated methods for integrating public input into transport planning, creating an increasingly democratic and responsive planning process. Though technology can increase the geographies and perhaps the speed and volume of public involvement, sometimes public involvement can extend project schedules or defeat projects, which I illustrate with an example from Austin (TX) in Chapter 5.

A changing climate for political budgeting

The social climate has had a profound impact on budgeting for transportation investments in recent years. As society's values and priorities evolve, so too do the focus and distribution of transportation funding. Sustainability, equity, public health, technology, and public participation all play a role in the political budgeting process.

With the growing awareness of climate change and its potential impacts, there has been a substantial shift in societal attitudes towards sustainable practices. This has affected transportation budgeting, with a greater proportion of funds being allocated towards environmentally-friendly transportation solutions. This includes investments in electric buses, bike lanes, pedestrian-friendly infrastructure, and light rail transit systems, which can all reduce the dependence on fossil fuels. Social justice movements of recent years, particularly the Black Lives Matter movement, have highlighted the systemic disparities in access to quality transportation. This has led to an increased emphasis on equity in transportation budgeting. The idea is to ensure that disadvantaged communities, which have historically been underserved by transportation planning, receive a fair share of transportation investments. This could mean better transit services in low-income areas, improving the accessibility of transit stops, or even subsidizing fares for those who cannot afford them. However, social justice remains a set of goals to achieve in many communities. The COVID-19 pandemic has also significantly affected transportation budgeting (Budd and Ison, 2020; Li et al, 2021). Transit ridership plummeted for public health reasons, requiring substantial subsidies to continue the services with limited funding from transit fares. To ensure the safety and health of the public, substantial investments have been made in sanitation measures, capacity restrictions, and contactless payment technologies. The social climate's openness to technology has influenced transportation investments too. With society's increasing acceptance of technology, more funds are being allocated towards intelligent transportation systems (ITS), autonomous vehicles (Guerra, 2016), and smart city initiatives (Angelidou, 2017). These investments aim to improve transportation efficiency, safety, and user experience, but also risk diversion of fundamental work to build and maintain basic transportation networks, including sidewalks (Ehrenfeucht and Loukaitou-Sideris, 2010; Wright, 2022). Increasing recognition of the importance of public participation in decision-making processes has led to a greater emphasis on public engagement in transportation budgeting. Participatory budgeting initiatives, where citizens directly decide on a portion of the transportation budget, have been gaining traction in many cities. In summary, the social climate greatly influences transportation budgeting, reflecting shifting societal values, needs, and expectations. As society continues to evolve, it's critical that transportation planning and budgeting adapt in tandem to better serve the public. One of these approaches is to think beyond the present budgeting cycles to enable longer-term planning of likely and desirable futures.

Critical realism's deeper truths for transport

These changes in technology and thinking take place in a political climate marked by polarization. Transport planners cannot remain neutral but must lead with facts and values they determine to support community goals, rather than carrying forward past practices and hoping for better results. This takes a critical perspective, critical realism (Næss, 2015; Bygstad et al, 2016), to be specific, looking at transport on the surface level of events, a deeper understanding of the mechanisms that lead to the events, and the underlying structures of law and economics that may or may not be immediately impacted by the transport planning process. This is not to claim that critical realism has a unique or complete access to truth. Indeed, some philosophers consider social constructionism and critical realism to be in conflict. However, Andrew Sayer suggests that some forms of social constructionism are entirely compatible with critical realism. He uses the example that Ronald Reagan once tried to challenge the social construction of 'battered women' by calling them 'runaway wives.' 'The only way the latter social construction can be challenged is by defending the realism, objectivity or practical adequacy of the first social construction: they really were battered' (Sayer, 2000, p 92). Taken together, this new understanding of transport futures more closely aligns the way planners produce and disseminate knowledge with the natures of the phenomena in question.

Legitimacy, accessibility, social learning, transparency, and representativeness encompass key issues for evaluating democratic planning in the 21st century. These issues related to planning processes do not always easily mesh with research on transport, which has tended to focus on quantifiable results that address important aspects of human transport systems, but cannot comprehensively address how the systems are planned, constructed, operated, and maintained by human actors—how the systems impact real peoples' lives in complicated ways. A critical realist perspective promotes empirical analysis of events to uncover causal mechanisms at both individual and city levels, which can support better understanding of the structures at play—while recognizing that they may not be fully observable. Figure 2.1 provides a simplified window through which each pane of the LASTR framework can clearly observe events changing over space and time, though causal mechanisms maybe obscured, and underlying structures may be difficult or impossible to discern.

Embedded in the approach of reviewing transport projects through these lenses is the notion that professional ethics can have an impact on

Figure 2.1: A window of legitimacy, accessibility, social learning, transparency, and representativeness for critical realist planning truths

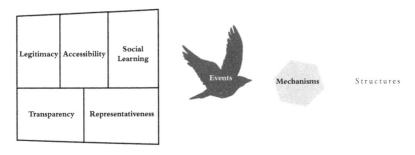

the choices made by individual actors and teams—planners, engineers, public administrators, and others—that impact people and resources. The next section provides a brief introduction to how each discipline approaches transport problems, and how that can impact the development of transport projects.

Assessing methods through transport codes of ethics

In the US, each major field of practice has a code of ethics to provide guidance on challenging quandaries that professionals face. Beyond helping practitioners to strive for excellence, they also provide bookends on acceptability of ethical work that may be used to discipline those who cross the boundaries. If the distinction of *what* practitioners do in their fields is difficult to separate from *how* they employ methods in their practice, then a review of professional ethics can suggest links between how a practitioner thinks they should perform their duties with a notion of what approach is appropriate in a given context. There are common threads and differences that run through the codes of ethics for the American Planning Association (APA, 2021), American Society for Public Administration (ASPA, 2013), and the American Society of Civil Engineers (ASCE, 2021).

Similarities between the fields approach to ethics address the public, professional integrity, competence and respect for law and rights. All three organizations stress the importance of serving the public interest. This involves ensuring that the work of planners, administrators, and engineers positively impact the communities they serve and does not cause harm. All three codes mandate honesty, integrity, and transparency in professional activities. They call for professionals to adhere to high standards of conduct, avoid conflicts of interest, and maintain the reputation and dignity of their respective professions. The APA, ASPA, and ASCE require professionals to strive for excellence in their work and to maintain and enhance their professional knowledge and skills. All three organizations emphasize respect for laws, regulations, and human rights, and require professionals to act in accordance with legal and ethical obligations.

Differences among the disciplines may be more instructive to help consider how practitioners differ in their work across their roles, addressing the environment, democracy, and professional development. The ASCE Code of Ethics specifically mentions engineers' responsibility to hold paramount the safety, health, and welfare of the public in all their professional activities. The APA and ASPA, while also emphasizing public interest, don't highlight safety and health to the same extent. The APA's code of ethics has a particular emphasis on environmental stewardship, urging planners to pay special attention to the interrelatedness of decisions and the long-term consequences of their actions on the environment and sustainability. The APA and ASPA codes stress the importance of promoting and facilitating public participation in decision-making processes, reflecting their focus on democratic governance and public administration. The ASCE Code of Ethics, while recognizing the importance of public feedback, does not have the same explicit emphasis on democratic participation. The ASPA Code of Ethics places a significant emphasis on the nurturing and development of upcoming professionals. While the APA and ASCE Codes also highlight the importance of mentoring and competence-building, the emphasis on professional development is especially strong in the ASPA Code.

If practitioners internalize a code of ethics in their work, then the differences between the fields highlight what methods are most likely to lead to success as defined by their fields. Engineers might analyze different designs to reduce the likelihood of a crash, even at the expense of the environment or livability, such as thinking that trees in a street right-of-way might produce a crash hazard, without considering the less direct health benefits to air quality or mitigating urban heat islands. Planners might favor analyzing long-term scenario-based approaches to future environmental challenges, while discounting more immediate needs of the community. Both planners and public administrators' emphasis on democracy can significantly slow transport projects, even if community insight's impacts on the process can be uncertain. Understanding more about how practitioners approach their work ethically helps highlight how they might be able to work more effectively together with these differences made clear. Further, this background helps consider how they might approach information and use of knowledge in transportation planning.

Artificial intelligence, bias, and prediction

Artificial intelligence (AI) poses a great prospect in measure with its risk. Innovations in AI are beginning to impact planning practice, especially

28

since the public launch of tools like visual Dall-E and text-based ChatGPT. Deepfake videos developed with AI could mislead the public about transport planning, along with any major democratic issue. AI magnifies problems with what we think we know about urban transportation planning, but these problems help us clarify approaches to seek truth in an era of misinformation.

Scholars have already provided helpful grounding definitions and charting of future possibilities, and we can expect an increase in research and debate on the best approaches to apply AI in transport planning. Thomas Sanchez describes categories of AI tools in planning practice as including machine learning, artificial neural networks, natural language processing, and computer vision (Sanchez, 2023). Machine learning can provide pattern recognition in large datasets, such as sentiment in community comments on planning issues through social media (Evans-Cowley and Griffin, 2012). Artificial neural networks emulate brain functions to perform complex tasks such as recognizing patterns to make predictions, which El Esawey and colleagues applied to make sparse bicycle traffic counts more usable for planning (El Esawey et al, 2015). Natural language processing attempts to derive meaning from words, such as Subasish Das and colleagues' work to mine YouTube to learn about consumers' notions of automated vehicles (Das et al, 2019). Computer vision can process visual data such as mapping sidewalk networks using satellite imagery (Hosseini et al, 2023). Sanchez characterizes some of the challenges to AI adoption in planning as 'fear and uncertainty, the need for new skills, changing data needs, unclear goals, transparency and explainability, bias, and ethical considerations' (Sanchez, 2023, p 4).

AI approaches in planning show great prospect and new challenges. Zhong-Ren Peng and colleagues describe the opportunity of intelligent systems for planning as rooted in the ability to process large amounts of information in a consistent manner, creating models to predict likely outcomes, supporting planners decision-making, facilitating public involvement, and supporting development of future scenarios (Peng et al, 2023). While Sanchez characterized the challenges to adopting AI in planning, Peng's group stresses a cautious approach, due to ethical concerns including adherence to the AICP Code of Ethics mentioned in the previous section. Most researchers agree on the bias problems in AI, which are not unique to planning. At first glance, it would seem that AI approaches could reduce bias in decisions because the programmed methods are consistently delivered, as opposed to a human approach, which can be partial to individuals and groups, inconsistent, lazy, or even maleficent. However, choices on which datasets are used for training inherently leads AI to conform to those choices, which may misrepresent underprivileged populations. Further, programmers' biases or that of their employers may be integrated into AI systems. Hence, any predictions that planning support systems with un-checked AI make are likely to be biased, with major ethical implications for practice.

For AI systems to be effective in supporting transport planning, they must have ethical checks. Translating a human-in-the-loop (HITL) concept to urban planning, Peng and team developed a typology of urban planning processes that forecast a four-stage development (Peng et al, 2023). AI-assisted planning includes a planner-in-the-loop, such as a planner leading processes, but using ChatGPT to develop and refine readable text for broad audiences, including translation. They describe AI-augmented planning as starting with a planner's needs to identify, forecast, or simulate urban issues with AI, then leading to a planning decision. AI-automated planning, however, would 'make plans based on the goals set up by planners,' where the planner reviews the AI output (Peng et al, 2023, p 7). A final phase of AI-autonomized planning would take planners out of the loop entirely, with AI developing plans through its own learning and decision-making methods. Expanding from recent research on the topic, Peng and team recommend engaging with marginalized communities and researchers about equity issues, working on trust and morality with how planners should work with AI while following ethical codes, protect privacy, develop expertise in AI and planning, and develop quality planning-related datasets to improve AI agents for planning. Truly, AI requires an expansive approach to meaningfully improve urban planning while supporting ethical human thriving. AI is only one of the many socio-technical issues changing what might be possible in urban planning, and how researchers and practitioners can understand what is true, what is good, and what is right. To do that, we need to take a step back from technology and think about what we think we know in the first place.

Aligning natures and knowledge

Researchers approach challenges carrying a background of knowledge and experience, influencing how they understand the reality of bicycling, what methods are appropriate for unearthing that reality, orientation towards what they think a 'good' solution might be, and individual reflection on their role in turning research into reality. Philosophers of science might use terms like ontology, epistemology, axiology, and reflexivity to convey these issues. Taken together, they may reflect a research paradigm that can frame how bicycling research is devised, turns into shared knowledge, and impacts practice. Table 2.1 introduces a framework to organize research purposes within a tradition, suggesting common types of data, research approaches, and a reference study.

Quantitative research that seeks to rationally test hypotheses and describe relationships between variables could be described as fitting in a positivist

Table 2.1: Frameworks for transport research in generalized categories

Research purpose	Knowledge tradition	Data	Methods	Example study
Describe or explain	(Post-) positivism	Quantitative	Surveys, experiments, or modeling	Marshall and Ferenchak (2020)
Explore, interpret, or describe	Constructivism or interpretivism	Qualitative	Interviews or ethnographic field studies	Lugo (2013)
Evaluate results	Pragmatism or critical realism	Mixed-method	Multi-method, observation or case studies	Hosford et al (2020)
Emancipate communities	Critical theory or social science	Participatory	Participatory action research (PAR) or community-based participatory research (CBPR)	Dressel et al (2014)

Source: Adapted from du Toit and Mouton (2013)

tradition, descended from Auguste Comte's philosophical project to re-center empirical evidence in seeking truth (Wyly, 2014). Derived from scientific approaches to the natural world, positivism assumes that context-independent rules underlying actions can be described through observable data, and that quantitative data from the past can help forecast a future—a very common approach in transport studies (Melia, 2020). However, a post-positivist approach recognizes that there are limits to how transferable evidence from known contexts are to unknown contexts. One such example is Ferenchak and Marshall's modeling of bicycle crash rates, bicycle infrastructure, and other variables across 12 US cities (Ferenchak and Marshall, 2020). Their study showed lower bicycle crash rates with more bicycle lanes, and that these infrastructure improvements were more impactful than just 'safety-in-numbers,' where drivers could be more cautious when sharing roadways with bicyclists. Despite their use of multilevel, longitudinal, and negative binomial regression models across 8,700 block groups, the *Journal of Transport and Health* published a critique based on the study's findings centered on the lack of evidence for causation—that the researchers could not show that the safety effect was driven by the bicycle lane infrastructure (Schimek, 2020). In a response, Marshall and Ferenchak re-iterated that they never purported causality, but that this approach to modeling nonetheless shows an association between bicycle infrastructure and reduced crash rates (Marshall and Ferenchak, 2020). There are some post-positive approaches that may support describing causality, such as structural equation modeling. However, they still will not explain *how* a transportation organization or other groups enact better outcomes—these approaches often involve understanding social processes through the people involved.

Researchers can deploy a critical realist approach to bridge critical evaluation of a transport problem towards emancipation of affected communities. Critical realism builds from a foundation of understanding about the nature of reality (ontology), how we can come to understand a limited portion of that reality (epistemology), and to what degree a finding impacts society in a good way (axiology). At its core, a critical realist perspective does not end an inquiry at the observation of events seen in a positivist approach, but searches for underlying mechanisms and structures that led to the observable events. In doing so, leading progenitor of the philosophy, Roy Baskar, identified what he called an *epistemic fallacy*, the incorrect attribution of an observed event as causing an observable change (Bhaskar, 2013). In reality, Baskar and critical realists argue, unobserved mechanisms and structures may have as much or more of a role in real phenomena. In social science, critical realists do not just seek to understand events impacting humans, but to uncover the underlying structures that led to any sort of human suffering—and thereby support human emancipation and thriving.

Given that critical realism is a nascent philosophy, there are few, but impactful, urban planning and transport studies taking this approach. In the 1990s, critical realists informed from earlier work in geography attacked theoretical approaches in urban planning theory. Banai suggested that the long-running rational comprehensive approach to planning had failed to incorporate the changes in sociotechnical-environmental relationships over time and space (Banai, 1995). This means that any given study showing a correlation between phenomena cannot be assumed to hold the same relationships in different contexts. Rather, Petter Næss argues that causal relationships between the built environment and travel can be characterized as 'tendencies engendered by generative mechanisms,' and that combining qualitative and quantitative methods to uncover the real mechanisms and structures that impact travel decisions (Næss, 2016). A critical realist approach would use the empirically-observable events as a flag of sorts that can indicate the actual causal factors underlying the observable events. Responding to critiques of a perceived ability to 'cherry pick their preferred explanations' in critical realist studies, Steve Melia developed an abductive approach to identify differences in transport spending in the UK at different times and resolve a research question, then retroduction to determine circumstances that would have prevented the same event from occurring (Melia, 2019). By moving between theory and evidence, then diagramming and revising causal mechanisms, the approach 'suggests that their different reactions can be traced back to underlying changes in social structures, as well as personal interventions of some key actors,' including economic ideologies as causal mechanisms that would not have been identified from a positivist approach (Melia, 2019, p 252). Further, Melia applied Baskar's critical realist model as a method to analyze political decision-making in transport, following a 'RRREIC+R' process of resolution of the research question, redescription of interviews, retroduction to identify causal mechanisms and structural changes, elimination and identification of explanations, correction through graphical description, and recommendations based on normative values (Melia, 2020). Despite the potentially valuable prospects of the critical realist paradigm for urban and transport planning, even the most recent work focuses on arguing for its use and sharpening its approaches, while recognizing other valuable approaches to complex problems remain (Waite, 2022). Though critical realism continues to expand its impact across disciplines and seas, studies on transport from this perspective have come from the UK, and not applied in American or African contexts, as provided in Chapters 5 and 6 of this volume.

Contributions

This chapter argues that approaches to understanding transport have changed over time to incorporate more data, more stories, more technologies, and more perspectives, but that none of them have fundamentally solved wicked sociotechnical problems, and offered only glimpses of more truths. Technologies cannot think for us. The LASTR framework, combined with a critical realist perspective, is this work's contribution to expand our capabilities of achieving good social ends through transport planning.

Transport planning's long-running dependence on economic rationality may have run its course, recognizing that models can only reflect the data they were input with, rather than envision futures and paths that expand human thriving and ecological balance. These tools are not redundant, but transport planning now keeps these approaches in their place—to test specific ideas created by teams of planners and collaborators that achieve desired ends—even if these may incorporate selfish interests and power struggles that continue to characterize the public investment milieu. Transport planning's increasing emphasis on access to destinations, rather than simple mobility, illustrates this complexity. Getting to a destination requires a choice of a travel mode on a given route, to a destination enabled by land use as a combination of economic, environmental, and social factors. Planners can feed models with data and public resources, but their impact on thinking and solving problems have limits.

This chapter also showed that attempts to simplify these complex problems through technological solutions such as dashboards may cause more harm than good. By choosing a simple set of metrics to analyze, such a technocratic solution actively re-directs attention from complex problems—the mechanisms and structures that created the challenges in the first place. Adding bigger datasets and more public discourse may not solve problems either.

The COVID pandemic has provided a global illustration of the interaction of global mechanisms and complex structures to impact society. To incorporate all of the issues relevant to transport planning, cognizant of the fields' disciplinary ethics, this chapter proposes the LASTR framework as a window to observe transport events, which then can be analyzed to produce and test theories through a critical realist framework. Before testing them on the two major cases of this book, however, the next two chapters peer deeper into the quantitative and qualitative approaches to understanding transport truths.

Box 2.1: Transport futures takeaways for practice

- Several transport traditions hamper decisions, including the use of economic rationality to build forecasting tools, causing a mismatch between what 'experts' think is likely to happen in the future and actual human behavior.
- Reducing individual and collective transport costs by improving access requires re-making planning systems designed to optimize speed and mobility.
- Crowdsourcing and other public input methods can be designed for early project guidance, rather than last-minute commenting.
- Providing transport data dashboards can simplify complex information, but system designers may not understand which measures are most critical for public access.
- Critical realism is a way of thinking about complex problems beyond the surface events, which practitioners can apply to wicked transport problems.
- Practitioners can design methods and evaluation approaches by aligning the issues to purposes and specific methods, as shown in Table 2.1.

3

Seeing Trees Through
Random Forests

This chapter describes three paradigmatic changes in quantitative methods for transport planning: big data, causality outside of laboratory contexts, and machine learning approaches. In contrast with other scholars, I argue that big data is not all data—digital transport traces track technological objects rather than people and their transport decisions. I show this through a case of understanding micromobility, where e-scooter trips may be fully tracked under a corporate subscription model. However, many owned vehicles, including bicycles, provide no digital trace whatsoever. Therefore, reliance on data from shared mobility services may mis-represent the broader population of users. Planners relying on these forms of potentially biased 'smart city' information could inadvertently prioritize users of specific mobility services, creating a negative feedback loop. As an example, a planner identifying unsafe intersections by calculating the number of crashes per bike share trip—rather than performing bicycle traffic counts throughout a city—could prioritize areas in the central city and along recreational corridors frequented by tourists over the city's everyday bicyclists. Tracking rental trips is not the same as all trips for any travel mode. Understanding the prospects and limitations of quantitative analysis in transport is critical whether working on an individual project or an entire forest of transport issues.

This understanding argues in favor of new methods of data fusion—combinations of representative surveys and other methods with big data to mitigate bias while maximizing spatial and temporal accuracy. Because transport is such a complicated problem, guided by human decisions, simplified models are often burdened with causality—turning one knob such as transit fees shows a concomitant behavioral change. Nevertheless, post-hoc studies show that models that rely on past assumptions consistently fail to predict the future. Machine learning is a set of approaches that may support more nuanced predictions through testing with multiple options and iterations, particularly when informed by structural equation models from measured behaviors. This chapter also endeavors to pull in a key concept from geographers that impacts the nature and predictability of transport models. Non-stationarity shows that relationships between variables such as price sensitivity or traffic congestion are not stable across a region. The proximity and adjacency of variables impact real behavior throughout the region, but this issue needs to be incorporated in practice, rather than remaining a field of scholarship. This chapter is intended to cool some excitement over recent advances in quantitative methods and chart a path forward for making transport methods align with reality and ethics. Part of these solutions includes technological advancement—programming research findings into digital planning solutions, and part is recognizing limitations of quantitative-only approaches. To see the forest for the trees, sometimes we have to deploy cutting-edge methods, but always think seriously about the impacts of our methods on transport planning decisions that can last generations.

Quantitative innovation in transport planning

Numerical approaches for transport research support a variety of study designs across application areas of trip estimation and safety analysis, with a large impact coming from innovations in machine learning. Computing resources and data availability have supported simultaneous increases in the spatial scale of models along with disaggregation of travel behavior. Machine learning methods, in particular, support analysis of an increase in classification, clustering, and prediction of variables and comparison of effects to test and expand possible explanations of bicycling travel behavior, safety, and improvements for sustainable transportation. Three innovations are leading this change: the use of 'big data,' understanding causality outside controlled settings, and the application of machine learning.

'Big data' refers to the vast amounts of information collected from our devices and infrastructures. However, it's important to note that this data mainly captures the activity of technologies, such as shared e-scooters, and not necessarily the behavior and decisions of individual users. For example, data from an e-scooter service can tell us how and where the scooters are used, but not why someone chose a scooter over their own bicycle, which leaves no digital trace. To get a fuller picture, we need to blend big data with traditional methods, like surveys, to balance broad coverage with a deep understanding of people's choices.

Understanding cause and effect in transport planning is another challenge. Traditional models might assume, for example, that reducing transit fees will increase usage. But transport is a complex system, shaped by many factors beyond cost, and these simplistic models often fail to predict future trends accurately. Liyu Wu and others designed a multi-modal, parsimonious model of bus, bus rapid transit, and metro lines fed by walking and shared biking with different cost assumptions (Wu et al, 2020). They found that the efficiency of providing the shared bike services reduced cost to individuals and the transit service providers, even suggesting that the cost of bike share systems could be paid by the savings to transit companies. In a novel combination of a field experiment with simulation, Ning Guo and a team in China experimented with high-density groups of pedestrians and bicyclists on a straight path and a ring-shaped path (Guo et al, 2020). The team calibrated traffic behavior scenarios with a genetic algorithm calibrated with video taken in different density and directional configurations. Bicyclist flow was highest in a uni-directional test, and without pedestrians, suggesting guidance for path design. Modeling can provide insights in scenarios that are impractical to test directly, such as designing different configurations of shared bike and transit networks. Transport studies driven by economic assumptions of travel behavior can build understanding of complex systems outside of a lab environment, but often fail to address the interactions of culture and technology that impact real systems.

These innovative methods are driving change in transport planning, but they aren't a magic bullet. It's important to understand their limitations and use them responsibly, balancing the insights they provide with ethical considerations and a grounded understanding of people's transport behavior. By blending technological progress with a human-centered approach, we can ensure that transport planning serves our communities effectively.

Big data is not all data

A general definition of big data involves the collection, analysis, and use of high volumes and varieties of data at a high velocity. In transportation, this could involve real-time traffic flows from GPS or mobile devices, additional mobile sensors, social media, and other data streams. Some purport that new transportation technologies that create big data—such as individualized trip records from ridehailing or transit—can improve safety and sustainability (Neilson et al, 2019). Big data from maritime cargo ships have enabled more sophisticated modeling than what was previously available (Peng et al, 2018). Big data can help track travel modes often missing from transport agency statistics, such as the use of crowdsourced bicycle trips (Griffin and Jiao, 2015b). Big data for transport includes more than just flows of people and goods. Social media produces huge corpora of language about transport, enabling advancements in topics such as transportation safety (Das and Griffin, 2020). When posted online or shared with the media, big data can support transparency in the transport planning process.

Some suggest that the new sensors and data flows enable digital twin modeling of transportation systems in hyperbolic terms, suggesting digital twins as 'a perfect candidate technology at present' (Gao et al, 2021, p 298).

However, big datasets that underly the digital twin concept only exist because of new products like smartphones and electric cars. If we trust big data sources to completely and accurately represent real transportation, then we miss any trips made without a given technology. As geographer Richard Shearmur critiqued the big data zeitgeist, 'however big the data, Big Data are not about society, but about users and markets' (Shearmur, 2015, p 967). Interview research with experts in big data reveal more biases and problems, and perspective for understanding the differences between big data and real society (Griffin et al, 2020).

Big data, perhaps ironically, needs to be aggregated and reduced for at least two purposes for transport planning (Griffin et al, 2020). Before individual trip records can be sold by big data providers, they are grouped to protect human privacy. Data providers also aggregate trips to protect business interests, such as freight carriers' cargo, specific routes, and delivery times. Additionally, most current travel modeling software requires aggregated data, often to a geography called a traffic analysis zone (TAZ) typically larger than a city block. All of these processes reduce the resolution of information in space or time. There are some spatial and temporal modeling approaches, such as Markovian techniques, that can help re-gain some of this lost specificity (Griffin et al, 2020). The data aggregation and reduction methods can fundamentally change the data, even if required legally or practically. Big data usually needs to be made small, just to be useful for transport planning.

Certainly, big data provides more glimpses into truths for transport planning. If big data is *most*, if not all data for transport, it could lead to greater representativeness than traditional approaches. It could also lead to more transparent planning processes, if the information were readily accessible. However, these questions have not been fully studied. *More* data may feed transport models' accuracy, but planning in democratic societies require some form of public input to be considered legitimate. Democratic planning requires making transportation data understandable to the humans that could be impacted by decisions. Small transport modes can make some of these big challenges more visible.

Descriptive understanding of micromobility

Shared mobility modes, such as electric scooters, are accessible to users to find with an online app because their GPS location is a built-in feature of the system. GPS tracking of the devices, and public access of the application programing interface (API) allows quantitative description of individual trips. Grant McKenzie leveraged this data from Washington, DC to be able to perform a descriptive comparison of e-scooter and bike share trips (McKenzie, 2019). In this pre-pandemic study, McKenzie found that even though the spatial use patterns of these two modes were similar, the temporal patterns of bike sharing member trips showed a clear commuting pattern with strong peaks in the number of trips in weekday mornings and afternoons, whereas casual bikeshare and e-scooter trips had single peaks in the afternoons, with more trips on weekends. Previous studies of bicycle counts show differences in use patterns based on their location, as well. In Austin, the Shoal Creek trail connecting the University of Texas and downtown had am–pm weekday peaks, showing a utilitarian pattern, whereas the east–west oriented trails and those along the city's reservoir showed a mixed-recreational pattern (Griffin and Jiao, 2015a). My early work with Strava and other crowdsourcing platforms showed over-representation by young adult and middle-aged males, and in high-income areas—biases that continues through later studies (Griffin and Jiao, 2015b; Roy and Nelson, 2018; Dadashova and Griffin, 2020; Lee and Sener, 2021).

There are many other studies that analyze spatial and temporal variation of micromobility trips to describe patterns of mobility. Quantitative data accessible from shared mobility modes' API, bicycle counters, and crowdsourcing smartphone apps provide detailed information to assess micromobility modes in recent years, which was not available before integration of these technologies. Despite technological advancements, transportation agencies have not deployed complete bicycle and micromobility counting systems the way they have for cars and trucks. The current state of research on the topic is to combine sparse counting data with many other sources of data to serve as a proxy for a complete traffic monitoring system for these modes. The latest combines bike sharing data with crowdsourced data from Strava and Streetlight with multiple variables on the local environment, including bicycle paths, household income, commuting data from surveys, and spatial variables like proximity to central business districts, which all factored, explained three-quarters of the variability in simple traffic counts (Broach et al, 2023). 'One thing that the process made clear is that, rather than replacing conventional bike data sources and count programs, big data sources like Strava and StreetLight actually make the old "small" data even more important' (Broach et al, 2023, p 14). This study, which used Poisson regression with K-fold cross-validation performed by eight of the world's top researchers in the topic and supported with funding pooled from eight transportation agencies, nonetheless made incremental progress in understanding bicycle transportation in the US. Critically, I suggest that the methods are too resource-intensive to be practical for planning practitioners to implement, and therefore offer little return on the funding agencies' investments. The gap between research and practice in big data to date is too far.

These data sources also show the biases discussed in the book so far. E-scooter trips currently cost similar to taxi fares, whereas a bicycle trip that does not pass an automatic counter is not recorded. Similarly, crowdsourcing apps depend on smartphones with data subscriptions and people willing to spend time recording trips. In this way, those with more expendable cash are more likely to be counted in these systems. There have been a few pilot studies on equitable bike sharing to help bridge the gap of access, especially in Portland (OR) and Philadelphia (PA) (McNeil et al, 2018; Dill et al, 2022). Despite some notable efforts to improve equity, financial and other barriers to bikeshare and e-scooter systems continue, imposing limits to the representativeness and legitimacy of gleaning these data types to understand micromobility in a city. Rather than adding more data to more sophisticated modeling techniques, the field should solve problems by re-thinking how we use observations to understand the causes of transportation system changes.

Causality and travel behavior

Though many studies suffer from an attempt to draw causal factors from correlations, quantitative methods offer several approaches that offer potential solutions. Randomized controlled trials (RCTs) are considered the gold-standard in causality (Hariton and Locascio, 2018), but difficult to apply with human subjects outside of medical research. The problem with RCT for travel research is that the variables involved are difficult to manipulate while controlling other real-world interactions. Bike lanes or congestion pricing zones apply to entire communities, making separation of treatment and control study participants nearly impossible, as opposed to simply giving a new medicine to a treatment group, and a placebo to a control group. Some policies and interventions, like e-bikes, can be given like medicine, however. In Sweden, frequent drivers were randomly assigned an e-bike, which led to an average increase of one bike trip per day, decreasing total car mileage by 37 percent (Söderberg f.k.a. Andersson et al, 2021). Given that an e-bike placebo would be easier for participants to detect than a sugar pill, the research team switched the treatment (e-bike) and control (no e-bike) groups after 5 weeks, which served two benefits. First, it helped motivate the control group to participate in travel surveys, and second, the switch supported internal validation of travel behavioral change. Results offer very compelling evidence of a strong impact of e-bike availability on travel behavior. Because people are unlikely to change their environments to participate in a study, another approach is needed to understand impacts of the built environment on travel behavior.

Natural experiments provide an opportunity to measure differences in travel behavior over time, usually while holding the location measured as a constant. This approach leverages changes that happen to the environment, like street construction or policy changes, as long a baseline data is collected before the intervention existed, or perhaps after an intervention is removed. The Mueller neighborhood in Austin (TX) was developed from an abandoned airport, creating an opportunity to study the role of a highly connected, walkable and bikeable community. Physical activity surveys before and after people moved to this neighborhood showed respondents reporting an increase in weekly physical activity by 66.4 minutes after moving (Calise et al, 2012). These initial results were limited by the fact that the neighborhood was largely incomplete—the first phase of residential housing was completed, but very little of the shopping and/or office destinations were built. A Texas A&M study team then embarked on a more ambitious natural experiment at the Mueller community, adding objective measures of activity with accelerometers, GPS, and travel diaries to survey methods. (I coordinated field work with this team during part of the study.) However, a 'major challenge emerged from difficulties in recruitment as we needed to identify case participants before their move from various locations that were not known to the researchers in advance and the contact information of these target participants was not directly accessible' (Zhu et al, 2022, p 10). Despite these challenges, the team did publish results using accelerometer and survey data that people who moved to the Mueller community (37 people in this study) averaged 76 minutes more of moderate-to-vigorous physical activity per week, as compared with 78 participants who did not move to the community (Lee et al, 2023). In a different natural experiment, Jennifer Dill and team seized on the opportunity to measure physical activity and bicycle trips taken by adults and children before and after the city of Portland (OR) installed bicycle boulevards that calmed automobile traffic (Dill et al, 2014). They found no statistical differences from the treatment, but recommended later studies consider differences in the length of time after construction to measure behavior changes. Another study on the introduction of bike sharing and e-scooter systems between the years 2012 and 2019 provided a large-scale natural experiment of travel behavior. We analyzed the differences in vehicle miles traveled before and after addition of these modes among 177 urbanized areas in the US in 2019, 69 of which had e-scooter systems, 88 had bike sharing, and 59 had both e-scooters and bike share. Difference-in-differences modeling showed cities with bike share would be expected to decrease daily per capita driving by 1.465 miles, but that introduction of e-scooter systems alone is not likely to significantly impact driving (Choi et al, 2023). Natural experiments provide an alternative to RCTs when the variables in question cannot be manipulated by the research team, nor can participants be assigned random treatments. However, natural experiments are fraught with challenges ranging from isolating changes from different causes, including entanglement between social, political, environmental, and technology impacts, and control over recruiting the right participants to join at the right time, and correctly follow the study protocols. For these reasons and others, researchers increasingly look toward new approaches with bigger data and faster computing to improve study speed and outcomes.

Machine learning for biased bicycling

Machine learning, a type of artificial intelligence that can learn and improve from experience, offers a promising solution for processing high volumes and frequencies of data updates. It can handle complex, multi-variable scenarios, testing and learning from many possible outcomes to make more accurate predictions. Machine learning approaches can process data in a systematic and comprehensive manner that humans could miss, but it will tend to solidify biases in the data used to train the algorithm. Transport planners and data scientists should understand the opportunities and challenges of machine learning approaches.

GPS and accelerometer data record a tremendous amount of information about travel, but finding a solid signal about what activities are tracked require significant processing. Machine learning often includes 'random forest' approaches that use machine learning approaches to identify the most important variable branch of a multi-variate model. Avipsa Roy and team demonstrated a machine learning approach to classify GPS and wrist-work accelerometer data that can successfully classify five different travel modes: walking, bicycling, bus, motor vehicle, and Vancouver's elevated, automated rail system called SkyTrain (Roy et al, 2020). This approach could increase the speed and decrease costs of personal travel monitoring, however I am not aware of direct comparisons with travel surveys at present. Similar approaches might also help identify appropriate variables to understand travel relationships, which could lead to new theories about the factors that shape travel.

Machine learning algorithms can support analysis of larger datasets and higher numbers of variables, adding to explanations of the variables that support bicycling. Researchers build machine learning models by developing training data with correct labels—which can be supervised or unsupervised—and then applying the trained algorithm to un-labeled data and evaluating the results. Tulio Silveria-Santos and others explored survey data with four machine learning approaches (Decision Tree, K-Nearest Neighbor, Random Forest, and Support Vector Machine), finding the Support Vector Machine optimized predictions of shopping by bicycle or kick-scooter (Silveira-Santos et al, 2022). Using performance metrics such as accuracy, precision, and model recall, the authors showed that machine learning can support bicycle research with a relatively small dataset. The classification role of machine learning can be particularly useful for summarizing large datasets such as GPS and accelerometer readings into trip modes. Similar to Silveria-Santos' study, Avipsa Roy and her team found the Support Vector Machine algorithm performed best in this task, classifying modes with a 90.9 percent accuracy (Roy et al, 2020). Machine learning methods can also leverage subjective insights, such as unstructured data from social media. Topic modeling of social media posts on dockless bike share using latent Dirichlet allocation (LDA) through Support Vector and naïve Bayesian models were not as accurate as the more traditional approach of logistical regression, however (Rahim Taleqani et al, 2019).

Several studies of crowdsourced bicycling data existed prior to 2020, but my colleague at Texas A&M Transportation Institute at the time, Bahar Dadashova, led our new approach to expand existing bicycle count data across the entire state of Texas called a mixed-effect, random parameter model. Starting with 80 possible explanatory variables, we built a regression tree with random effects to account for unobserved spatial and temporal variation. The model then split variables based on their paired importance in explaining bicycle traffic counts, predicting counts to a 29 percent margin of error (Dadashova and Griffin, 2020). This approach expanded both the geographic scale and variety of explanatory variables over previous work. However, we noted that 'the modeling effort may be too resource-intensive to apply in many transportation agencies at present' (Dadashova and Griffin, 2020, p 18).

This approach supports descriptive research about bicycling in a post-positivist paradigm, but knowledge about interpretation, evaluation, or emancipation may require qualitative methods. Sophisticated modeling approaches including machine learning can obscure biases, rather than solving them. Instead of pushing agency leaders to devote more time and resources to simply counting vulnerable traffic modes, these modeling methods incorporate big data biases related to income, gender, and neighborhood in the explicit variables, and in the unobserved 'random effect.' Given the huge gaps in data gathering over the state, this biased dataset produced biased results, but I argue that these are better than having no statewide knowledge about bicycle traffic volumes. Such a huge place as Texas is an excellent place to study another confounding problem in quantitative transportation data: sometimes places vary because of their distance from other places, rather than other variables.

Spatial heterogeneity, or, 'everything has its place'

Geographers know something that most planners, engineers, and many of the world's top transport researchers are unaware of or prefer to ignore: proximity matters. Since people stroll, fly, roam, bike, and meander, a single trip is impacted by multiple places along the way, and the places closest to the traveler probably impact them more than those far away. Or as Waldo Tobler invoked in a first law of geography: 'everything is related to everything else, but near things are more related than distant things' (Tobler, 1970, p 236). If you were to join me for a walk in San Antonio (TX), and we pass a native mesquite tree, the most likely tree we pass next will be a ... mesquite. If we hiked together long enough, we would pass by different tree species, perhaps in increasing frequency. Depending on the time we walked, we might even get hungry enough to crave a fajita taco, which is traditionally seared over the hottest flame with a sweet smoke from mesquite wood. In this way, the spatial arrangement of one phenomenon also impacts the likelihood of another related phenomenon, and maybe that partially explains why San Antonio is not known for its borscht.

This related variation of phenomena by space is why transport planners should listen to geographers when it comes to quantitative analysis. Most of our fields' models are 'global' in the sense that a single formula is developed for each geographic unit of analysis—be it a street block, census tract, or state. Global models ignore variation over space, assuming conditions in one corner of the analysis area must be the same as the other corner. As transport geographer Harvey Miller described, 'disaggregate spatial statistics such as local indicators of spatial association (LISA) statistics (Anselin, 1995), the G statistics (Getis and Ord, 1992) and geographically weighted regression (Brunsdon et al, 1998) capture spatial association and heterogeneity simultaneously' (Miller, 2004, p 284). To offer one non-food related example, descriptive analysis of environmental variables with a global, ordinary least squares regression model explained over 40 percent of the variation in crowdsourced bicycle volumes (Griffin and Jiao, 2015b). A Moran's I test showed the dependent variable, bicycle kilometers traveled, was spatially autocorrelated, which led me to perform other tests, and to use a geographically-weighted regression (actually a different equation for every block group in the study area) that explained over 75 percent of variation in bicycling trips logged in the study area. If I have been bold to suggest that many transport fields are missing the place, if not the point, then I must also be meek enough to step back into using our disciplines' codes of ethics to examine if we agree on what is right in the first place.

Assessing quantitative methods through transport codes of ethics

Transport practitioners using quantitative methods have an ethical, disciplinary obligation to perform truthful work, even when projects are complicated, budgets are tight, and political pressures significant. Civil engineers must be able to relay to 'clients and employers if their engineering judgment is overruled where health, safety, and welfare of the public may be endangered,' implying evaluation of their recommendations against these public goods—though these need not only be merely quantitative. Engineers, planners, and public administrators' codes of ethics all require continual professional development to apply current methods that provide the most accurate results. For public administrators to 'provide accurate, honest, comprehensive, and timely information and advice to elected and appointed officials and governing board members, and to staff members' (ASPA, 2013), they also must deploy the most appropriate methods including quantitative approaches. Notably, that list did not include members of the public—their obligation for democratic participation is to 'inform the public and encourage active engagement in governance,' though, they are required to be open, transparent and responsive to the public. Engineers and public administrators' codes speak to issues of the present, without specifically addressing issues of the future, as planners' code does. For planners aspire to 'have special concern for the long-range consequences of past and present actions,' and 'pay special attention to the interrelatedness of decisions and their unintended consequences' (APA, 2021), they must be able to evaluate the likely impacts of transportation decisions for future generations. Planners also are charged to 'identify the human and environmental consequences of alternative actions including the short and long-term costs and benefits,' suggesting detailed tabulations of likely scenario outcomes. Each of these transport professions have an ethical obligation to deploy quantitative methods to serve the public, and transport plans, by definition, impact the ways that people access the city, and region, perform and seek services, including building friendships and families. In transport planning, quantitative methods can make the difference between the status quo and a better life for many people over generations. Doing the right things and doing things right are both important.

Contributions

This chapter demonstrated approaches to see the forest and the trees by use of advanced methods, including random forest machine learning. Transport planning is largely rooted in quantitative, rational approaches to understand past, present, and future issues. However, historical lessons from Chapter 2 demonstrated the value of storytelling—both to explore possible desirable futures that a quantitative forecast might not suggest, and to connect with the lived experience of people and the politics that form key drivers in transport decisions. Nonetheless, quantitative approaches continue to drive much of the innovative thinking shaping better transport planning methods, and hopefully, good decisions.

This chapter showed ways that availability of big data for transport planning, and new machine learning approaches to find meaningful patterns in the data can support new knowledge for transport planning. However, big data inherently excludes people who do not purchase or use the items that leave the data traces, whether through smartphone apps or purchased transport services. Hence, representation is the key challenge of using big data for transport planning. At the same time, shared mobility services enable understanding of emerging travel modes more on par with motorized vehicles, which transport agencies support with extensive monitoring and modeling programs.

To understand transport truths, the field must engage beyond seeking larger transport datasets to think through how to derive causal knowledge aligned with observable changes in the transport environment. Randomized controlled trials remain the gold standard in evaluating causal impacts, but require experimental constraints that are not often possible. Natural experiments and quantitative approaches including differences-in-differences can provide methods when control and treatment groups can be separated, at least in time. Short of causal approaches, correlational methods can help describe relatively unknown transport phenomena, like crowdsourcing bicycle volumes in recent years. Correlational approaches to planning that incorporate the likelihood of phenomena to be similar to nearby measures are able to deal with spatial heterogeneity, or change in variables due to geography, rather than other causes.

Finally, this chapter connected research to practice, by demonstrating practitioners' obligations to leverage the most appropriate methods to solve problems in the public interest. Public administrators' codes largely relate to the organizations they serve, rather than the public directly. Engineers are required to attend to public health, safety and welfare, even when it counters their previous assessments. Planners have to aspire further for future generations, leveraging quantitative and other approaches to assess likely impacts of transport investments through forecasting or other future-oriented approaches.

Recognizing that quantitative methods form the basis of the field, this chapter also demonstrated that the high-buzz approaches such as big data are subject to the same logic as a single intervention on a single person. Transport planners must engage with a variety of methods, and remain open to partners across disciplines to achieve the highest opportunities now and in the future. Despite these opportunities and warnings, transport planning is perhaps now more than ever, open to exploring new and different approaches to finding truths that serve ethical and good goals to pressing challenges.

Box 3.1: Quantitative takeaways for practice

- Big data and sophisticated modeling methods can create 'black boxes' that perpetuate biased knowledge and reinforce inequalities in the built environment.
- Natural experiments and careful research design can support knowledge about transport changes that cause changes in travel behavior.
- Thinking like a geographer can help uncover the impact of regional and local spatial variation on transportation.
- Transportation forecasts are value-laden and involve bias, with ethical obligations to consider the impacts of transportation plans on existing and future communities.

4

Why and How Matter Now

This chapter provides antidotes and warnings of the limitations of quantitative methods through qualitative innovation. I sequence case examples to determine how qualitative insights might be used in a transport study or plan. The first case involved developing an interviewing protocol spanning an ocean—students from Texas working with a team from Republic of The Gambia to support planning for increases in tourism in the West African country. Using the same partnership, I describe how a public participation geographic information system (PPGIS) can be used in online and paper-based formats to scale local knowledge. Next, I show how qualitative coding can be used to organize themes and concepts for research and practical applications, arguing that these methods are under-utilized by practitioners for turning public comments into practical guidance. As a capstone for qualitative research methods, I summarize a small-scale case study of a two-decade planning process for a pedestrian bridge in a socially contentious setting in Texas. This chapter positions futures storytelling as a critical method for transport planners, using cogent and impactful examples from the Greater Philadelphia Futures Group. If contextual match is an advantage of qualitative methods, assessing findings is more of a challenge, which this chapter supports through reflective guidance on the limitations of reliability and generalizability and the time and resource requirements of qualitative study. Finally, the chapter shows how to assess qualitative analysis from the ethical framework, showing how the approach supports the multiple levels of analysis from a critical realism ontology.

Qualitative innovation in transport

Transport planning has always involved qualitative analysis, especially talking with people. Engineers, politicians, landowners, community members all have something to say about how streets and walkways, vehicles, parking, and the problems and solutions involved in each should be addressed. More recently, digital tools like Google Street View enables almost ubiquitous photographic imagery of streets in many of the worlds' urbanized areas. Conversations, images, sounds and video—basically any data that is not already tabulated into a strictly numerical format, is qualitative data. Qualitative methods are not the same as qualitative data, however. This section briefly introduces some of the newer qualitative approaches to uncovering truths in transport, while recognizing that qualitative data can be analyzed with quantitative methods, and vice versa.

Data collection and analysis tools provide the means to gather qualitative data such as a sound recorder, and then to organize and analyze the information such as in qualitative analysis software. In addition to sound recording interviews or focus groups, transport planners often use ground-based and aerial photography, analyze textual content, and perform observational field research, recording data on a clipboard or other tools.

Qualitative geographic information systems (GISs) include a variety of methods to store, organize, retrieve, and visualize textual, photographic, sound and other information that is tied to a specific location. Qualitative GIS is also inherently quantitative, in the sense that the qualitative data is digitized and georeferenced into a spatial and numerical grid for mapping and analysis. By geo-locating qualitative information about transport, GIS as a practice and method inherently engages with truths about lived experiences and the environmental surroundings of transport. 'When different data sources and methods of analysis are played off each other and collide in different ways, they result in complementary, contradictory, or subtly nuanced and intersecting multiple truths, each of which can be thoroughly explored to foster more robust explanations' (Cope and Elwood, 2009). In a Montreal-based study, researchers performed interviews while walking through a neighborhood, gaining perceptive and sensory insights from participants as they walked (Battista and Manaugh, 2019). The researchers then geo-located the qualitative data in a GIS with other measures of the built environment, gaining insights on the individual and group factors that impact how people make decisions about walking. If nuanced understanding of places involves more complicated data than zeros and ones, then our methods should be able to analyze rich and layered variations across spaces.

While a doctoral student at the University of Texas at Austin, I was fortunate to take Talia McCray's Built Environment and Public Health class, which influenced how I understand the ways in which we can work with communities to gain insights on travel that are unobtainable through typical surveys and other datasets. A different study leveraged a social media platform for endurance sports, Strava, to understand how the environment changes how runners consider and communicate running approaches (Martin et al, 2023). Researchers initially tried to group characteristics of running segments by length, slope, elevation, proximity to population, and land cover, but they could not develop reliable categories of these quantitative measures.

However, use of runner's online comments about these running segments with qualitative analysis by the research team resulted in a classification system of codes, or labels, that included 'urban, scenic, natural, grind, and track.' In so doing, the researchers conclude that qualitative analysis is just as important in an era of big data as previously. Coding qualitative data can help organize and assess textual, photographic, and other data, but this analysis does not by itself prioritize topics for urban planning. Interview, group facilitation, and survey approaches with knowledgeable subjects are necessary for gaining imaginative insights on planning topics.

Delphi technique can be a particularly valuable approach to exploring transport futures, gaining insights from experts through either a face-to-face discussion or survey approaches. Delphi processes involve addressing a problem with a panel of experts, whose composition is critical to achieving insights that connect likely and desirable futures (Okoli and Pawlowski, 2004). In transport, that might include leaders of community organizations, experienced planners, politicians, and business leaders. A facilitator asks each of them a series of questions, and then uses responses—which might be quite divergent—to refine a next round of questions that are iteratively summarized to eventually reach consensus on the problem at hand. The problem of understanding how to implement improvements likely to lead to increasing the mode share of bicycling in a city is a key example. Researchers built a panel of 28 experts from the Netherlands and New Zealand from professional practice, policy, advocacy, and research backgrounds, who identified infrastructure changes as a prerequisite to mode shift, followed by value of promotional programs, changes in governance, socio-cultural and contextual and individual factors (Adam et al, 2018). This study's findings created a hierarchy of action based on logic, which many quantitative studies measuring effect sizes cannot directly address. Essentially, they were able to construct and revise a conceptual diagram of actions leading to increased cycling mode share. This process shows how researchers addressing urban transport problems may be inclined to continually study problems in-situ, considering the drivers and bicyclists, for instance, as the object of study. However, by talking to the people involved, researchers can unearth planning processes and propose a hierarchy of interventions that create change where it is needed—in the planning workrooms and civic halls where large and small urban interventions are hatched. If urban transport is to be an inclusive field that serves entire communities, then its analysis cannot be hatched and led by elites.

Participatory approaches emphasize the people most impacted in communities, and can be informal and reactive in practice, and well-structured and replicable for research. As a transportation planner in the Austin (TX) region, I balanced seeking on-the-ground input at public events, and using then-new online social media approaches to gain insights to inform our board's transportation policy and funding decisions. Hosting an event in front of Austin's city hall, I learned the value of charisma and charm in working with communities. I had the fortune to work with an elegant professional communicator, who people gravitated towards and initiated conversations, while I was able to dig into the details of our agency's proposals with visits. Though public input at contrived events can effectively engage communities, qualitative researchers also embed themselves in cultural sub-groups to identify changes and inequalities in the daily lived experience of transportation. Adonia Lugo's ethnography of urban bicycling and social equity in Los Angeles delves into how social processes effect outcomes, through the role of the CicLAvia open street event (Lugo, 2013). As a participant-observer and interviewer, Adonia Lugo is able to 'witness shifts in cultural attitudes toward mobility' (p 203), exploring insights from bicycle advocates that are not available through other research methodologies. Qualitative approaches tend to acknowledge the role of a researcher and may address issues of internal validity by aligning constructivist or interpretivist theory and method. Qualitative research can address the complexities of how knowledge and action are constructed through social processes, lending insights into how to change transport organizations and processes.

Pragmatically, organizations combine quantitative and qualitative information in making decisions, and therefore mixed-methods research can work with the complexities of both approaches. For instance, Kate Hosford and colleagues evaluated a popular typology of bicyclists (Geller, 2009) through surveys and interviews, showing that only seven out of 25 interviewed cyclists identified as fitting in one of the system's four categories. This emphasis on how things work in the real world, as opposed to the researchers' perspectives, supports evaluation of business-as-usual bicycle planning approaches, and may help address persistent challenges. Case studies may be the most common way to evaluate project outcomes, and often use descriptive statistics to quantify the scale of a challenge, and then qualitative analysis to expound on the case's specifics (Akar et al, 2012). Critical realism is an emerging conceptual framework that recognizes that only some layers of socio-political processes are directly observable, and therefore knowledge is context-dependent and limited (Næss, 2015). Critical realist research approaches recognize differences in observability between immediate events (like adoption of a bicycle plan), underlying mechanisms (like a transportation organization's funding process), and structures (such as cultural norms that influence elected leaders). Critical realist studies can 'provide deeper explanations for policy change than existing approaches used in transport studies,' but are not yet common in transport research (Melia, 2020, p 285). Pragmatic and realist approaches to transport research are focused on understanding, but other approaches can support direct change.

Participatory action research (PAR) directly involves community members and researchers in a collaborative project to improve bicycling outcomes, rather than just observing and recording results. Sometimes called community-based participatory research (CBPR), the researcher often seeks a supporting role to help address a community's challenges, and cedes control of the process and outcomes. Researchers worked with community groups to address poor air quality and health outcomes in a low-income, urban community in Milwaukee, Wisconsin, with direct and indirect impacts (Dressel et al, 2014). Immediate impacts included repairing bicycles and facilitating group rides. Over the longer term, the team built capacity for the bicycling community to continue these efforts, including parents modeling healthy behaviors for children—potentially with long-lasting benefits. Lasting change often takes extended engagement, however. Community engagement for the Milwaukee study spanned three summers, which may be considered quick from the perspective of research powering community change.

Each of these studies serves a different research purpose, aligning a tradition of knowledge with appropriate data and methods. Though these studies were chosen for their relatively clear approaches within each tradition, bicycle research often spans and connects these traditions because of the interconnected nature of impacts between disciplines. Bicycling research may be centered in a discipline, but it shares the interdisciplinary connections of geography, engineering, social, and environmental issues. Researchers can strengthen their approaches by connecting to these disciplines when appropriate and considering how their position may impact the research process (Rose, 1997). Recognizing the situated nature of knowledge supports a strong study design, whether it is centered in quantitative, qualitative, or mixed method approaches. Interviewing is a fundamental method for qualitative research, and it can be useful for triangulating quantitative knowledge as well.

Cross-Atlantic interviewing for tourism transport in The Gambia

'Seeing tourism through the lens of a true Gambian himself helps identify what tourism looks like for someone who lives there,' reflected an architecture student after performing an interview with a local tourism worker and university student. In Summer 2021, as the globe struggled to find new normal protocols for engagement and teaching amid the pandemic, my department chair approached me with the opportunity to teach an online planning workshop on sustainable tourism with students from the University of The Gambia (UTG) and the University of Texas at San Antonio (UTSA). UTG students were principally studying business and tourism, while the UTSA students were largely in architecture and planning programs, further adding complimentary skills.

Despite the contextual differences between the state of Texas and The Gambia, students shared the same language, lived in large cities, and communicate frequently with smartphones. In 2021, Gambians had 101 mobile cellular subscriptions for every 100 people, higher than the average 84 subscriptions per 100 people across Sub-Saharan Africa (World Bank, 2022). The first assignment for UTSA students was to conduct a remote interview with a peer from the University of The Gambia, which I hoped would build rapport, cross-cultural understanding, and some technical skills in conducting interviews with specific questions and purposes in mind. Interviews were conducted most often over text messages using WhatsApp, but also some voice calling, email, and video call. I asked UTSA students to adapt my suggested questions for interviewing through semi-structured interviews, which addressed topics of the Gambians' interest in tourism, description of a place in The Gambia they would like international visitors to see in the future, a problem for tourism, barriers for small business, and advice on how the Texans can support sustainable tourism in the project respectfully.

Though the main draw for international tourism at present is similar to other West African nations 'sea, sand, and sun (we call it the triple S)' as one Gambian student put it, UTG students reported several different destinations that they would like more visitors to see. One destination was Tumani Tenda. A UTG student described it as:

> a village inhabited by people of the Jola tribe, with a community managed camp. At this village, tourism is practiced responsibly with the future in mind. Visitors will experience rich African culture in its natural surroundings whilst contributing to the development and livelihood of the local people and the environment. Locally sourced resources are used in very creative ways to not only provide comfort to visitors but to also protect nature.

Others mentioned some of the more famous sites, such as Kunta Kinteh island, part of a UNESCO World Heritage site at the mouth of the Gambia River that served as both the beginning of colonial enslavement and its abolition. A UTG student also mentioned Kiang West National Park, which includes over 11,000 hectares of savanna, woodland, tidal flats and mangrove creeks along the southern banks of the Gambia River.

Gambians mentioned problems and concerns for the country's tourism industry. Access to destinations, particularly further outside the urban areas, hampers tourism. A Gambian student reported that the road network, at present, does not support visitation to many rural sites. The country's official statistics confirm this challenge, showing 28 percent of the road network is paved, as of 2021 (Gambia Bureau of Statistics, 2021). The strong seasonality of travel is also a challenge, with the wet season of the Sahelian climate occurring between June and October (World Bank, 2021), overlapping the May to October peak tourism season of European travelers. Also, UTG students reported that much—one student estimated 80 percent—of the international tourism is from pre-paid packaged trips, so that most of the cost stays in the United Kingdom or other countries that organize the packages. One UTG student mentioned a potential solution to this problem could be a licensing agreement that requires the tourism organizers to 'retain and reinvest [a] certain percentage of their earnings in The Gambia.' UTSA students' questions about how they can best work with UTG included hopes that our combined effort would be shared so that the university could persuade the government to support tourism more. The class's report and other information is available on the course web page (Griffin, 2021).

Public participation geographic information systems for local transport knowledge

As part of the same project with UTG, I drafted a public participation geographic information system (PPGIS) survey to demonstrate a way to identify opportunities and constraints for sustainable tourism development in The Gambia. I drafted a five-question geographically-specific survey and emailed UTG students with a brief invitation for them to share the survey with others and invite responses. The survey prompted respondents to choose a location on an interactive map and respond to the questions Figure 4.1 is a screenshot of the geographically-specific comments made by Gambian tourism students and professionals.

This approach to public engagement, particularly for remote projects, supports several components of the LASTR framework presented first in Chapter 1. Since the survey gathers input from simple prompts, it compiles legitimate knowledge from the community. Though the prompts do seek to direct a topic for the response, the open-ended nature of the prompt encourages any input the respondent feels appropriate to share. The survey's geographic and descriptive precision is limited only to the skills and knowledge of the respondent. Accessibility, particularly in the Gambian context, is limited to internet data which may require additional, paid access. However, one could argue that such an approach is much more accessible than a public meeting, mailed survey, or other engagement method. This demonstration project was not designed to transparently support knowledge of the process, how the data would be used, nor the results, and therefore did not directly support social learning. To deploy a similar project to support these goals, the PPGIS should link to a live map of responses, which ideally would also include contact information and guidance on how to evaluate whether the results were being used. Respondents could learn from each growing response, and potentially contact others for additional

Figure 4.1: Survey results of an online demonstration: Public Participation Geographic Information System (PPGIS) for sustainable tourism in The Gambia

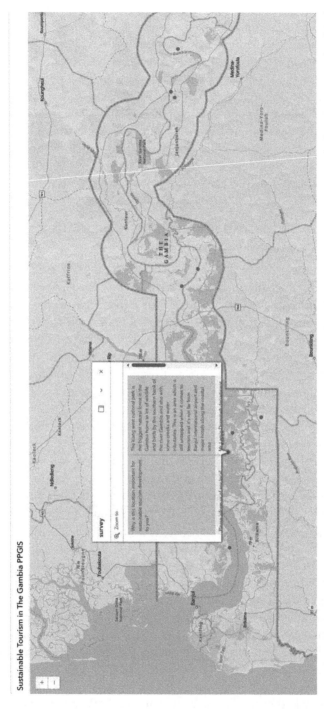

Note: The text reads: "[Question] Why is this location important for sustainable tourism development to you?"; [Response] The kiang west national park is the biggest national forest in The Gambia."

Source: © Esri, 1995–2024

communication if an option for sharing contact information were provided. The survey did include a single question on the respondents' home district, which enables a basic evaluation of representativeness by population. A more comprehensive approach would consider key representation issues for a project, such as ethnic background, gender, age, or other social grouping. Class discussion on the survey suggested students understood how such an approach could be deployed at scale as part of a comprehensive public engagement process. In these ways, interviewing resulted in much more than a description of context and relationships—the method built a foundation that enabled iterative understanding of how the groups could work collaboratively, within the limits of distance and technology.

Thus far, this chapter has only introduced interviewing and a PPGIS questionnaire approach to collecting qualitative data for transport planning. A metaphor for qualitative understanding might be how transport agency heads seeking project leaders would set several years of experience in transport, given that they have developed contextual knowledge about likely problems and solutions in a wide variety of situations. In short, they have developed a rich, sensory understanding of how people, machines, and geography interact to address access and mobility—they have qualitative knowledge. For transport experts to learn insights from others, they process qualitative information from people, places, and experiences, some of which can be online. Given the wide array of approaches to gathering large corpora of qualitative data, the next section addresses machine and human-driven processes to analyze what it means for transport planning.

Why coding matters in the age of natural language processing

Qualitative research is fundamentally about deep engagement with rich information, which supports knowledge consideration of context, action, and responses for transport planning. Coding as a research approach bridges from potentially large qualitative datasets, such as interview transcripts, photographs, journals, observations of participants, and more to a pointed research question. The *Coding Manual for Qualitative Researchers* describes a code as 'most often a word or short phrase that symbolically assigns a summative, salient, essence-capturing and/or evocative attitude for a portion of language-based or visual data' (Saldaña, 2016, p 4). Assigning codes to qualitative data engages a researcher in a process of personal knowledge of a dataset and challenging thought, as to which parts of the data are most important to address a research question. Recently, artificial intelligence and natural language processing approaches enable analysis of bigger qualitative data, faster. However, it has yet to be seen whether these approaches lead to greater human understanding of the issues or action given new knowledge.

Large qualitative datasets, such as the thousands of tweets analyzed in a study of how social media can be deployed for directed and passively-collected forms of public engagement in transportation (Evans-Cowley and Griffin, 2012; Schweitzer, 2014), pose a challenge for both human time needed to evaluate responses, and retaining an even approach to natural human biases in how to use the information. Natural language processing approaches such as sentiment analysis allows rapid psychometric evaluation of emotionally-charged, neutral, and other linguistic approaches that result in a clean and quantitative statistical evaluation. However, delving into what the responses mean for transport planning—such as why neighbors might be upset about a proposed rail line—requires closer reading, thinking, and analysis. A full-scale, traditional qualitative analysis might involve attributing tags, or codes of meaning, to public-contributed comments. A research team described challenges of hand-coding large qualitative datasets: 'You've got 500 codes first and then you've got notes everywhere all over them' (Jiang et al, 2021, p 94).

All this manual pouring over reams of transcripts, observational data or field notes is not replaceable, however, if a researcher is to develop a rich, bottom-up understanding of participants' insights about a transport phenomenon. Researchers who perform open coding on qualitative datasets can remain open to the theoretical meaning and impact of the work, allowing inductive theory-building that is grounded in the participants' qualitative contributions. In addition to traditional 'post-it note' approaches to qualitative coding, qualitative software tools such as NVIVO, Dedoose, and GIS can aid in the storage, retrieval, and visualization of the information and coding results. Abigail Cochran is a transport researcher using qualitative methods to unearth and share transport experiences of people living with disabilities. She applies a multi-stage coding process that identifies sections of text relating to her research topic, and then queries her coded dataset for qualitative data that connects concepts addressing a research question. For instance, 'to examine how respondents experienced stress, or a lack thereof, during social interactions when using different transportation modes or services, the coding process allowed for comparing excerpts in which "stress" co-occurred with "social interactions," as well as codes such as "bus" or "App-based ridehailing"'(Cochran, 2020). Whether supported by printouts and scribbles or the latest qualitative analysis software, researchers working closely with the data through coding methods support deep understanding and inductive thinking that lies at the heart of qualitative research.

Despite the challenges facing approaches that attempt to hybridize machine and human qualitative analysis, recent research on using new qualitative approaches suggest there may be ways 'that honor serendipity, human agency, and ambiguity' of in-depth human analysis, while leveraging some of the speed and power of AI (Jiang et al, 2021). Jialun Jiang and team's interviews with qualitative researchers showed frustration with often-messy analysis methods of software, paper, and personal engagement with team members about coding and analysis. Yet, respondents were also hesitant that developments in AI would remove a key part of the qualitative knowledge-building process, even if new approaches might address some of the challenges with organizing and quickly coding qualitative data. Following their suggestions, qualitative research for transport that incorporates new tools should also embrace the uncertainty of the qualitative analysis process, allowing researchers to deeply learn, struggle, and gain knowledge about cases that matter for transport.

An exploration (not peer-reviewed) of using ChatGPT to code a large text corpus of Google reviews of police stations suggests that human use of AI may be useful for some qualitive work (Flahavan, 2023). Following trial and error with developing a ChatGPT prompt, the AI was able to categorize reviews following human definitions for seven categories. Reviewing a sample of 50 manually, he assessed that ChatGPT categorized 44 reviews correctly. Some of the errors related to ChatGPT mis-categorizing sarcasm, a well-known problem with natural language processing tools. Notably, Flahavan had to provide ChatGPT with a complete guide and coding system, and so this is not building theory from individuals' qualitative insights; it is a simple content analysis that effectively categorized textual reviews and counted them. Even if this is not an example of rich insight, it may provide time and resource-strapped practitioners a quick method that may be better than no analysis. Similar approaches may help inform research and development of better tools and workflows for transport planning, as well. Perhaps in the near future, AI can help organize or speed rigorous qualitative research, while keeping it just messy enough.

Though this book cannot provide a how-to guide to qualitative transport research, these introductions to traditional and technological methods provide a glimpse into 'why and how' questions matter. Many transport projects have large financial investments, involvement of many complex community and industry groups, and their sheer complexity makes differentiating causes of delays impossible because so many factors overlap and intertwine. Hence, the following example of my work to understand how it could take 20 years to develop a small pedestrian bridge can offer some qualitative insights into how the transport planning process can go wrong—and how to right it.

Walking through a case study on a pedestrian bridge to understand time

A pleasantly cool morning in September 2014, dozens of elementary students in a low-income suburban neighborhood in northeast Austin (TX), bicycled across a just-finished pedestrian and bicycle bridge to Hart Elementary. Staff from the city's Safe Routes to School program guided them safely, and several of the ride leaders had a role in completing the project. The previous semester, students in this neighborhood had to take a school bus or were driven—since the only other route crossed the creek along Interstate 35, a 1.5-mile diversion considered too dangerous for children. Many of them received bicycles, locks, and helmets through a donation program, and were taught to ride safely by licensed instructors. The main connecting streets had just been transformed from wide, straight thoroughfares built for cars, to include a two-way cycle track—a bike lane protected by plastic barriers to designate a wide path on the street (NACTO, 2014).

This reasonably straightforward project had cost about a million dollars to construct, including over a mile of connecting bike lanes and signage—comparatively small for a city with an annual transportation infrastructure budget of US$86 million (City of Austin, 2014). The project's apparent benefits, including increasing physical activity, reducing school busing costs, and connecting a low-income neighborhood to destinations without requiring cars—belies the reality that the project took 27 years to complete, 19 years after funding. Adding a bicycle and pedestrian bridge over a creek in a park connecting two neighborhoods, when funding is already available, is usually straightforward for elected officials and the city staff supporting them (Wray, 2008; Handy and McCann, 2011). However, the city wrestled with addressing the problem for almost three decades before it was built. Active travel projects may be delayed for various reasons, including communicative issues such as a failure to communicate the project need, local opposition, and a lack of trust between actors within a project.

To delve into the impact of public involvement on the eventual completion of the North Acres Park bridge, I used 15 individual data sources (Griffin, 2018), including a detailed interview with the lead project planner, transcription of a council meeting that included arguments from all major sides, historical memoranda from the city, online media from neighborhood stakeholders, news coverage, and other government documents. A three-stage coding strategy was applied to analyze the corpus of qualitative data, including descriptive, exploratory coding, action-oriented coding through gerunds, and process coding content that supported and delayed the project. Coding provided a means to categorize and search the corpus of materials focused on causal action and foster the project timeline and analysis development. Concurrent review of case materials, including City of Austin meeting minutes, Internet pages, and interview data supported final coding review, including changes to coding and description of preliminary findings based on any discrepancies.

This study showed three phases of the project, pertaining to public involvement. Developing concepts and leadership (1987–2006) included the original project associated with city bond funding that originally authorized in 1984. The project would connect a major north–south bicycle route on the east side of the city while connecting the elementary school and shopping areas south of the creek with dense housing and a large park on the north side. However, the Rundburg Lane corridor north of Little Walnut Creek had developed a reputation as a haven for criminal activity. One neighbor to the south described the creek in a city council meeting as a 'natural barrier' that would be essentially broken with a pedestrian bridge's addition. As the project was discussed more, the southern neighborhood used its newsletter to voice opposition, 'based on the high crime rate on the north side of the creek versus our very low crime rate, one of the (if not in fact THE) [emphasis is original] lowest crime rates in the city' (Heritage Hills Woodbridge Neighborhood Association, 2007). This concern with crime is often associated with the apparent issues of personal security but also with a real or imagined change in property values over time. Confronted with a planning proposal contrary to their preferences, some neighbors took a 'not in my backyard' (NIMBY) approach, which has been described as a 'social response to unwanted facilities' (Schively, 2007, p 255). This type of reaction is typically associated with land uses such as factories or adult-oriented businesses. A planner I interviewed surmised, her experiences with delay in some similar projects tended to snowball 'because the longer it was drawn out, the more players came in. People moved in the neighborhood, found out about it, and ... you have these new sets of opinions of people with every opportunity for the project, and it's problematic.' To build trust with the neighborhoods, she decided to 'put the project on hold, so that the project can be discussed within the 2-year planning process. And so, that was a concerted, purposeful, like, I wanted the project to stop.' After taking so many years to date, Patty saw 'no reason to force this project.' This decision marked the beginning of rebuilding trust with the neighborhoods and a transition in perspective on the project towards one that more genuinely sought local perspective on the best decisions for the neighborhood.

What I call the public involvement phase began in 2007, when the lead planner obtained contact information for local stakeholders in the southern neighborhood that had expressed opposition from the project's previous files. Based on neighborhood safety concerns, initial discussions with these stakeholders, mostly over email, showed strong resistance to the bridge. Resistance from the southern neighborhood representatives was so strong that 'And THEN we, at one point, through the neighborhood planning process, we decided ... to make a concerted effort to reach out to the community on the north side of the bridge—that apartment community.' The Rundberg corridor's reputation for crime had been substantiated through a federally-supported grant to try innovative methods to reduce crime (City of Austin, 2016), and tension surrounding the bridge project continued to mount. 'Kids should not be walking through there,' wrote one commenter among 124 supporters of a Change.org petition, which the neighborhood association to the south produced (Heritage Hills–Woodbridge Neighborhood, 2013). The city adjusted the project design to include lighting and barriers to restrict access under the bridge abutments to address some of the security and safety concerns.

After 27 years of deliberation and planning, staff presented the construction contract to the city council for approval on May 14, 2014, marking the final project phase toward completion. The bridge's final design called for a 180-foot long steel and concrete bridge that is 14 feet wide. The trail connecting to the adjacent streets would be a bit narrower, with 10 feet of concrete. The city council item to consider the contract was moved to accommodate more than a dozen speakers that had signed up to speak about the bridge, with pleas both for and against, each using their blend of logic and emotion. Citizen arguments against the project sometimes aligned with a 'NIMBY' perception, stating, 'the bridge and trail are disproportionately large, too large and will dominate the park ... The unattractive bridge and trail is all that visitors to the park will see.' Many pointed out the more functional problem of what might happen to the school bus service. One phrased the issue as increased risk for both personal safety and school performance: 'they could get hit by a car and possibly killed ... Due to these children's socioeconomic background, they may or may not have other transportation to school, causing them to become behind in school.' Some attacked the staff's claims regarding the public involvement process overall: 'What is—what does that even mean, "significant public outreach"? Who were they out reaching to?' Several people also spoke in favor of the bridge, including bicycle advocates and a resident who wanted access to shopping south of the bridge and had few other options for transportation. Following detailed questioning of city staff on all of the issues, Council Member Riley motioned to approve the contract, and all voted in favor, except then–mayor Lee Leffingwell. Following approval of the bridge, city staff added a re-allocation of the wide residential roadway space to include a two-way on-street trail. Painted like a separate path on the edge of the existing roadway with plastic sticks as a buffer from cars, 'protected bicycle lane', designs have been associated with both reduction in crashes (Lusk et al, 2011), and increased perception of safety that encourages women and children to bike on roads they might previously not (Dill et al, 2015).

This case study demonstrated a case for considering social learning, legitimate public participation, and representative engagement. All groups showed evidence of social learning, but the impacts from these changes were not entirely predictable. Neighborhood residents explored their abilities to resist and impact the project. Politicians learned to empower planners to invest time and resources to engage with diverse communities. Almost 30 years passed with the continued delay on the project until the correct alignment of staff, leadership, involved citizens, and perhaps even culture change aligned. The lead planner's discussion of the importance of trust was confirmed through the neighborhood's opening up to a discussion about what the right solution occurred at the right time when she had halted the project to consider the neighborhood plan. The records uncovered in this study revealed no contact with citizens on the northern side of the bridge until a Spanish-speaking planner had the idea of holding a pizza party in the apartments serving the low-income community. When city planners failed to involve all those affected by the project, the individuals involved either chose to ignore others' perspectives or did not have access to knowledge about those with different points of view. Building trust with all community groups, including Spanish speakers, demonstrated legitimacy of the project. Finally, representative engagement supports the alignment of community goals. Even when faced with city staff working to implement the project, local homeowners organized effectively to sway power to change their environment. Whether their concerns were more related to personal safety or property values is somewhat irrelevant to this case—they skillfully deployed communication technology and rational argumentation to accomplish their goals. The homeowner's association began using web-based communication tools to organize against the bridge's construction several years before the city deployed similar methods to support a broader engagement initiative. As triangulated in this study through multiple sources, city staff eventually encouraged this type of approach, increasing representation and eventual completion of the project.

The original project proposed in the late 1980s was a pedestrian bridge over Little Walnut Creek to complete bike route #57, and the completed project almost three decades later fits that definition. This short case study shows how public involvement can pose delays and risks to project completion, though the end result is more likely to foster social learning, be deemed legitimate and representative of the involved publics. Extensive public involvement may not always lead to consensus, but it can lead to a better understanding of a common truth.

The case of the North Acres Pedestrian Bridge shows how a qualitative researcher can understand transport projects from the recent past, or currently under development. However, qualitative narrative approaches also provide tools to imagine and communicate transport futures.

Storytelling about the future: Greater Philadelphia Futures Group

Planning deals with multiple dimensions of uncertainty. As the previous sections explored, public involvement, politics, and budgeting practices add layers of ambiguity about planning processes on top of the larger issues of macroeconomic, climate, and social changes. Over 20 years ago, Martin Wachs argued that technocratic projections of the future through forecasting was not an adequate approach for planning to guide communities (Wachs, 2001). Planning based on a forecast from the past is perhaps the best way to continue with the same problems, and avoid course corrections that could guide solutions.

In Philadelphia (PA), a Futures Group composed of subject matter experts meet and share diverse perspectives to envision futures for the Delaware Valley Regional Planning Commission (DVRPC, 2023). Every 4 years, a sub-set of that group deeply engages in composing stories about these futures to help guide the region's long-range plan. Scenario planning provides an alternative approach to a single forecast, enabling attention to a wide range of possible futures and the levels of uncertainty of topics, it deals with interactions between complex systems and questions that might otherwise be ignored, considers what happens following crises, and requires analysts to address details of these interactions and identify key choices (Goodspeed, 2020).

The Futures Group analyzes local and global forces likely to impact the region over the next 25 years, and composes detailed stories in the form of future news stories, like this headline from the year 2034: 'The Impacts of Congestion Pricing One Decade In' (DVRPC, 2020, p 59) and 'Push for Programmable Roads as Carbon Tax Dwindles' in 2036 (DVRPC, 2020, p 72). The group votes on different forces they consider to be at play during the plan timelines, and arranges them according to perceived uncertainty and impact for the region, then identifies relationships between those topics to construct more detailed scenarios that guide the long-range plan.

We may have to wait until 2034 to determine whether DVRPC's scenario planning helped them chart a better direction than those relying on forecasts, but the approach has succeeded in bringing together disparate interests with serious thought about their collective futures, and how to use their thinking to help guide the region's plan. Scenario planning helps address the problems of uncertainty around futures by acknowledging that more than one transport truth exists in the present, and that many different futures are possible. Charting what is likely, and what is desirable, can help communities envision and take steps toward achieving a better future.

The narratives about Philadelphia's futures and how the underlying forces are likely to impact the events addresses both observable events and the mechanisms that cause them, enabled by socio-technical-economic forces. The next section introduces how critical realism provides a framework to understand complex systems at play in transport.

Reliability and generalizability of qualitative knowledge

In any kind of scientific research, the ability to know whether the study could be replicated with a similar process and results is important—this is referred to as reliability. Similarly, studies that provide meaning beyond the cases in the study are said to be generalizable. To the extent that transport research has traditionally been quantitative, qualitative researchers should attend to issues of the replicability of their work and how applicable their work may be to other situations, or perhaps to professional transport practices. Sometimes these concepts are conflated with validity, including how valid the approach can establish a chain of evidence (construct validity), and whether that validity could differ based on perspectives of those among the people under study (internal validity), versus those outside that group (external validity). In Ottawa (CA), academic and community partners worked together to 'ensure equity was an integral part of the proposed Transportation Master Plan update' (Linovski and Baker, 2023, p 174). The community organizations helped formulate the problems, work approach, and evaluating results as an equal partner with the researchers, described as participatory action research (PAR). In PAR, the researchers cede some of the power for these research roles, and prioritize community goals above the research itself. A PAR study design builds internal and external validity into the process, to the extent that community partners and researchers communicate their intentions and methods, and come to consensus on the validity of their approach.

Reliability can be quantified, even for qualitative data. Krippendorff's alpha is a traditional measure of the reliability for content analysis with multiple researchers, measuring a proportion of disagreement between coders ranging from zero for complete disagreement to a perfect agreement of one (Krippendorff, 2011). Our coding of a small number of interviews with experts in big data for transport research resulted in more than three-quarters agreement (Griffin et al, 2020). Though sufficient for this small study, this reliability statistic can help qualitative researchers review whether more data (interviews in our case) were needed, or if the coding constructs may be incomplete or poorly communicated among the research team. Reliability can be assessed with other methods, including refutational analysis involving analysis of real or hypothetical cases that would potentially refute a construct, and by constant data comparison to see how additional cases might change a developing theory.

Generalizability is not always the goal in qualitative research. Particularly for transport research cases, which may be large, complicated, and expensive, deep knowledge of a single case is valuable and may impact many people. In other words, a case need not be generalizable to be useful. However, Bent Flyvbjerg's study of an attempted traffic reduction and urban renewal project in Aalborg (DK) famously showed that a single case may nonetheless be generalizable (Flyvbjerg, 1998). Through selection of a critical case, Flyvbjerg was able to falsify the theory of rational decision-making based on economic knowledge, finding that 'one can often generalize on the basis of a single case, and the case study maybe central to scientific development via generalization as supplement or alternative to other methods. But formal generalization is overvalued as a source of scientific development, whereas "the force of example" is underestimated' (Flyvbjerg, 2006, p 228). For those seeking a more structured approach to generalizability, it may be assessed as a holistic concept of how a study's theoretical construct may apply to other concepts, or it could be assessed similar to reliability by systematically sampling results from multiple cases.

Issues of reliability, generalizability, and validity point to the extent to which researchers can say that a given answer is correct for the situation. Though sometimes painted in studies as independent from values and morals, these issues all connect with different perceptions of what is deemed right and wrong. Qualitative methods must also then be viewed from an ethical perspective.

Assessing qualitative methods through transport codes of ethics

Qualitative data and analysis for transport planning may be most powerful, and popular in use, when it engages with the personal and social worlds of people affected by transport. In practice, this means that interviews, photography, and observational data are likely to be useful research methods for the field, which have ethical ramifications regarding privacy, personal agency, and representativeness.

Privacy is a key issue with interviews, especially when datasets are shared or quotations are used in reports. Civil engineers are bound to 'keep clients' and employers' identified proprietary information confidential' (ASCE, 2021). Similarly, planners' code of ethics requires that information gained in a context considered confidential should not be disclosed, or used to the planner's advantage (APA, 2021). However, planners also must not 'deliberately fail to provide adequate, timely, clear and accurate information on planning issues,' which could in some instances require disclosure of confidential information. Public administrators' code does not speak directly to privacy, but their requirement to 'fully inform and advise' elected and appointed officials might obligate them to share information from the community up to their bosses, but not back down from leadership to the public (ASPA, 2013). Given these differences, three hypothetical transport professionals from each discipline could end up treating personal information differently while staying within their prescribed codes of ethics. If each were to interview community members (not a client) about a transport plan, the engineer and public administrator might publish quotes without asking permission, whereas the planner would have to clarify with the participant whether they intended to share the information publicly.

Agency of the participant or subject of research is also key. Public administrators' obligation to advance the public interest might center the benefit of the community over the individual, and a person's contributions may be included or excluded from the transport planning record based on a perceived impact to the planning process. Planners' code of ethics requires 'not engag[ing] in private communications with planning process participants if the discussions relate to a matter over which we have authority to make a binding, final determination,' which may be intended to prevent coercion, but could prevent a planner from engaging directly with some community members who might be most impacted by a decision.

Representativeness can be related to the concept of generalizability in qualitative transport research. When considered through codes of ethics, transport professionals of each discipline have to consider whether their qualitative research addresses the community of interest. In the previous section, careful choices of case studies provide opportunities to be able to generalize beyond the case at hand. However, common transport planning practice does not afford the opportunity to be able to choose case studies. Since practitioners do not often choose the projects and contexts they work in, they have to apply qualitative research to understand the communities at hand. They can incorporate mixed methods approaches to be able to weight, resample, or contextualize the qualitative insights, in order to be able to have the results represent the community ethically.

Contributions

This chapter showed how qualitative research is necessary to be able to understand critical cases and individuals' perspectives that drive how transport gets planned and is used in practice. In short, interviews, photography, focus groups and other tools provide deep understanding and rich insights that in many cases can be more powerful than quantitative tools when depth, rather than breadth, is necessary. As an example, San Antonio students were able to interview Gambian students to gain individual insights that led to knowledge about the role of transport and sustainable tourism as the country works towards a sustainable economy. Despite challenges with internet access and data fees, students used agile modes of communication, including text messaging, video conferencing, and e-mail. Through qualitative research they built rich understanding of each other, and were able to highlight differences and challenges in planning and development that might have been difficult, if not impossible, to discover with other methods. The PPGIS survey approach also showed that a simple tool can be geographically specific, allowing researchers to ensure that they consider the location as precisely as those who are contributing can provide the information. Even though this sample was small, students gained an appreciation for the volume of data gathered in a qualitative research project, and which technological solutions are beginning to support high quality, replicable, and timely research.

Qualitative research has a large toolbox of software and hardware tools to support data collection, storage, retrieval, and visualization. AI, specifically natural language processing, may provide a suite of tools on the forefront to support qualitative research in transport. At present, however, the most useful AI tools in qualitative research support dictation or other simple tasks. If induction is the critical theory building process that's enabled by qualitative research, then AI tools are not yet providing support for this type of research at least as shown by the work to date. However, hybrid approaches that leverage this strength of AI such as applying human coding schemas across large corpora of qualitative data could allow researchers to increase the speed, accuracy, and potential impact of qualitative research in transport.

This chapter also provided an illustrative example of the use of qualitative research to understand the recent past, and to explore possible futures. In the small pedestrian bridge project in Austin, the qualitative research project process was able to uncover the mechanisms that caused the delay of the project in addition to its eventual completion. As the slow development of the pedestrian bridge in Austin (TX) showed, planners and community leaders have to address the social challenge of transport planning with the complex logic, personal trust and care, and political and financial resources to solve problems. The Philadelphia-based comment narrative exploration of likely futures allowed their regional planners to explore possibilities that could not be foreseen or communicated from quantitative models. More powerfully, this type of collaborative envisioning creates teams and coalitions of thinkers about the future, which can support transport planning directly and through community networks.

Finally, this chapter explored some of the opportunities and problems of how we know what we know through qualitative methods. For qualitative research to make an impact on a largely quantitative field like transport planning, reliability, generalizability, and ethics need to be centered in transport research and practice. Questions about why and how transport systems work as they do have to be explored with qualitative approaches. If nothing else, this chapter shows the importance of qualitative research and has introduced some of the ways that it can be most impactful. In the next chapter, qualitative research is used to explore one powerful, evolving case with one of the largest and most impactful transport infrastructure features at our disposal: an interstate freeway.

Box 4.1: Qualitative takeaways for practice

- Interviewing is a fundamental qualitative technique for research and practice, and can leverage interactive technologies to deepen understanding.
- Qualitative coding targets human perception of language and visual data towards key research questions.
- Qualitative communication and analysis is key to understanding transport from communities perspectives, and to collaboratively imagine likely and beneficial futures.
- Planners, engineers, and public administrators can think differently about practical ethics, and should confront these differences for the public good.

5

Confronting Wicked Problems
in Austin, Texas

How do transportation planning organizations' narratives guide discourse and results? This chapter shows how agencies merge quantitative forecasting and policy stories while building advocacy constituencies, revealing more of the underlying real *transport social structure* proposed from a UK context (Melia, 2020). Informed by critical realism, this study clarifies the mechanisms that lead to *neo-advocacy planning*, a concept developed by Gavin Parker and Emma Street as a response to the challenges of planning in neo-liberal contexts. In this chapter, I use the term neo-advocacy planning as an inverse of public opposition to agencies, where government agencies strategically leverage community groups through organizational communication that supports public opinion for their leaders' dominant lobbying and voting constituencies.

'No tolls on existing roads' read one of many hand-written protest signs at the public meeting of the Capital Area Metropolitan Planning Organization (CAMPO)—the intergovernmental transportation group for the fast-growing Austin, Texas region. Crowds had gathered in a cool and dark auditorium in Anderson High School—moved from the normal small meeting room on the University of Texas campus—for the board's October 2007 vote on whether to include five toll roads in the region's transportation plan. Some shouted threats of 'political suicide' to the elected representatives on the board, led by then-state senator Kirk Watson (Wear, 2007). As a regional transportation planner for the organization at the time, I primarily analyzed land use and transportation data, and staffing events like this were also part of the job. Tension in the room was not a by-product of the context, but was created by the protesters as the years-long efforts of transportation planners, engineers, politicians, lobbyists, environmental activists, and community members finally condensed into public action.

The CAMPO board voted to approve all five toll roads that evening, but Senator Watson recused himself from the vote on expanding US 290 East from Austin to Manor, Texas, citing a conflict of interest because he had an ownership stake in a bank that supported development along that corridor. A deft public speaker and longtime former mayor of Austin, Senator Watson quickly moved forward for the vote that would invest over $1.4 billion for tolled highway expansion between the central city and surrounding farm and ranchland. Laws and guidance keeping transportation planning decisions public made actions more transparent while suggesting there were deeper levels of actions and hidden rules that were less plain to see.

Fifteen years later, the five toll roads have been implemented with successive phases and other projects. Toll roads are built and operated by the Texas Department of Transportation and the region's Central Texas Regional Mobility Authority—the latter had a 2021 net fiscal position of over $636 million, enabling financial leveraging for transportation projects throughout the region (CTRMA, 2022). Tesla's global headquarters and Gigafactory anchor new development in the region's southeast edge, near the intersection of two tolled highways—SH 130 and US 71 East. Throughout this time, the region's central corridor of Interstate 35 remained largely untouched, even as local alternatives including light rail were approved, but the proposed Austin and San Antonio commuter rail service—the Lone Star Rail District—was defunded and collapsed in 2016 (Jefferson, 2020). Despite transportation being the largest contributor to climate change in the nation (US Department of Transportation, 2022a), planning for mobility in Texas' capital region remains largely committed to cars.

Interstate 35 in Austin, Texas is both a material resource—a product of social structures and investments—and a locus of inter-generational debate about the future of the city. I-35 is the second most congested road in Texas, 'where it's always rush hour' (Texas A&M Transportation Institute, 2021), and a 'real and imagined socioeconomic and racial divide' (Herrick, 2008, p 2715). Both claims are truths. Solutions to remedy them diverge, with a state-driven vision of vertical and horizontal expansion to add capacity for mobility, and a local concept to reconnect the city by burying and capping sections of the freeway to 're-stitch' the city together.

In a 2022 forum of mayoral candidates, Texas House representative Celia Israel addressed the challenge of expanding the Interstate (Panjwani, 2022):

> I-35 is another example of a city that has not gotten beyond its racist past. It has divided us for too long. I do want to reconnect East and West. But I don't want to do it at the expense of us becoming another Houston and the Katy Freeway example, where we just build more lanes and expect that we're doing good things. I want the best.

Campaigning for his successful run for mayor of Austin, former Texas Senator Kirk Watson responded that 'we need to start with the understanding that it's not Austin's road. And so when it's not Austin's road, that means we have to work to get the best result that we're able to get.'

Beyond the political importance of such an investment in a key technology hub, federal, state, and local funding and concomitant public engagement requirements require vetting of ideas and expenditures (Meyer, 2016). The magnitude of investment and change in this project reveals more of the social structures and causal mechanisms of transport planning than are typically required in projects with less community impact.

This chapter shows multiple 'truths' in transport planning, in which data and information are targeted toward key audiences of politicians, funding agencies, and publics, to direct billions of dollars in investment along mutually exclusive and irrevocable pathways. The complexities of context, resources, actions, and results are obscured by ideologies, logical biases of the observers, and intentional obfuscation of actors. Critical realism offers a philosophy of science that recognizes that empirical information only includes observable phenomena, an actual domain is knowable but not always visible, and that reality remains hidden, but is a precursor of what we consider to be actual or empirical (Bhaskar, 2010; Walsh and Evans, 2014). This approach is particularly apt for studying planning processes, where a casual observation shows key events and facts, but the machinations of politics and obdurate professional methods are more difficult or impossible to discern.

To move past these challenges, this study adapts an approach to understand political decision-making in transport, Melia (2020), to identify mechanisms of rational response and public opinion. This study questions how transportation planning organizations' narratives guide discourse and results by comparing the counterintuitive cases of TxDOT's 'I-35 Capital Express' planning for the quickly-approved 'North' segment in Williamson County, just north of Austin, with the contentious 'Central' segment through Austin.

From hunting trails to three-story freeway

Before its growth into a tech capital, Austin remained a relatively quiet seat of government and home of the University of Texas. The city straddles two physiographic zones at the Colorado River. The rich soils of the Blackland Prairie supported crops and easy building sites, flanked by steep hills to the west leading upward to the rugged Edwards Plateau spanning central Texas. Generations of indigenous tribes and colonists used this natural corridor connecting Waco-Springs in the north, Barton Springs in what became Austin, to San Pedro Springs in San Antonio, beyond the edge of the Balcones Uplift to Del Rio Springs near the banks of the Rio Grande (Erlichman, 2006). Military funding from Spain extended the *Caminos Reales* to Laredo (circa 1700s), San Antonio, and San Marcos, and military funding from the Republic of Texas (1836–45) and the US Congress catalyzed the development of a rough north–south Military Road between San Marcos and Preston via Austin and Dallas (Erlichman, 2006, p 244). Following the increase in shipment of agricultural products along the corridor and popularization of auto ownership in the early 1900s, the corridor was expanded into a two-lane, paved Pan American highway connecting Mexico City to Dallas and further north by 1936. Though still a capital of a rural, agricultural state, Austin's position on this highway connected the city for trade and rapid growth to follow.

The growing state capital and university city of Austin did not differ from its Southern peers in terms of racism, however. A 1928 comprehensive plan for the city, followed by a 1931 zoning map, segregated residences and resource availability by race and income (Congress for New Urbanism, 2015). Coupled with discriminatory lending practices for home mortgages, made infamous through redlining of predominantly brown and Black neighborhoods as poor investments (Rothstein, 2017), East Austin was already on the road to a fully segregated portion of the city with a wide, grassy median shown in Figure 5.1 along East Avenue separating the community—before the highway was even built.

Before the nation's interstate system, the 'I' in I-35 meant 'Interregional' in the Austin area, and the Interregional Highway was a four-lane facility

Figure 5.1: 1930 photograph of East Avenue looking south from 12th St.

Source: Ellison Photo Co. [Item #C02070], Austin History Center, Austin Public Library

70

north and south of the city (Erlichman, 2006). In 1946, the city council decided to purchase land along East Avenue and further south after the state highway engineer DeWitt C. Greer 'frankly told them that "if you don't want the East Avenue highway, say so, and we'll quit and spend our money elsewhere",' leading to the city council affirming their purchase (Weeg, 1946). The highway department built the first section of the highway (then called US 81) along the East Avenue alignment by July 1952. Project construction was slow, but the gas tax in Texas was raised to 'five cents per gallon in 1955' (Erlichman, 2006, p 203), expanding the revenue stream.

On President Dwight D. Eisenhower's signature, the Interstate Highway Act of 1956 changed the game for transportation. This new stream of federal authority and funding, supported in part by a national fuel tax, transferred tremendous city-building autonomy from locally-elected city leaders to state highway departments (Brown et al, 2009). This response to recovery from the Second World War, ostensibly to provide rapid deployment of troops and equipment as a cold war advanced, launched a freeway building boom that would connect the nation's ports, cities, and many remote communities with a seamless, high-speed network. With visionary cues from Germany's Autobahn, interstates were designed with increasing automobile speeds with capacity to suit decades of growth in demand for trucks and private cars. Funding was 90 percent federal, so states clamored to contribute a tenth of the cost for huge projects with immediate payback in construction jobs, with the increased traffic anticipated to deliver permanent windfall of commerce across economic sectors. By 1975, the Interregional Highway had six main lanes, and was double-decked through the constrained right-of-way in downtown Austin. Construction and business leaders enjoyed the beginning of a huge and long-lasting windfall, while local residents and businesses lost their homes to the state through eminent domain proceedings. Austin's freeway came at a cost, but among the ostensible benefits was safety.

Interstates allowed entrance only through high-speed entrance ramps with large-radius curves, enabling smooth merging at freeway speeds. This restricted design also enabled spacing entrances to minimize conflict points and congestion, while creating speculative land value at exit points for gas stations, restaurants, and new residential and commercial development. Critically, the rights-of-way were often several hundred feet wide, with grassy medians to create buffers minimizing the potential for collisions with opposing traffic. The spacing also allowed later expansion of lanes toward the center, with concrete barriers in the center and guardrails at curves and exits, all designed to minimize damage from high-speed crashes that began to plague US communities.

A side effect of the entrance and safety features was a loss of access across the interstates. Construction of the freeway in Austin meant that communities previously connected with cross-streets could no longer access areas of the city without a long diversion to the next crossing. Daily commutes within Austin and similar communities were lengthened. Walking to the city's downtown was no longer feasible for eastside residents. The state's capital, university, and most of its employers were on one side of a long-term construction project, with eastside communities—more often brown and Black—now experienced segregation as a physical partitioning of the city. Even in studies of smaller city street contexts, heavier traffic and higher speeds sever communities. Donald Appleyard's path-breaking studies in San Francisco demonstrated neighbors had fewer social ties on busy streets, and in this way, Austin, like many other cities of the time, was divided by government action—the grassy boulevard dug out for steel-reinforced concrete—built on top of the cultural and legal barriers preventing full access to the city. Before I-35 was completed, the city had become fully segregated. Figure 5.2 shows the freeway's current context, looking south by southwest toward downtown.

With no major changes on the freeway over 40 years of rapid growth, business leaders, commuters and elected officials furthered a call for re-considering the highway's future. TxDOT proposed three separate projects on the same freeway, spanning sections called North (18.5 km from Round Rock to north Austin), Central (12.9 km through the center of Austin), and South (16 km through and south of Austin). The North project 'proposes to add one non-tolled high-occupancy vehicle managed lane in each direction along I-35 from SH 45 North to US 290 East. The project

Figure 5.2: I-35 facing south by southwest in 2023

Source: Author's own

will also reconstruct bridges, add a diverging diamond interchange at Wells Branch Parkway, add pedestrian and bicycle paths, and make additional safety and mobility improvements within the project limits' (TxDOT, 2023b). Similarly, the South project 'proposes to add two non-tolled high-occupancy vehicle managed lanes in each direction along I-35 from SH 71/Ben White Boulevard to SH 45 Southeast. The project will also reconstruct bridges, add pedestrian and bicycle paths, and make additional safety and mobility improvements within the project limits' (TxDOT, 2023c). The Central project is shorter in length, but the most urban in context. Initial review of the project did not determine that it would not have a significant impact on the environment, and so a detailed Environmental Impact Statement is required. Table 5.1 lists key information about the projects, showing the geographic scope of the sections are similar, but the context and anticipated cost for this project is quite different.

The resulting approval process for the environmental documents is counterintuitive. The simpler, less expensive, North and South projects that only required an environmental assessment took only 243 days and 255 days, respectively, to approve. TxDOT approved the Central project EIS 29 days faster than the South project, even though its scope is many times greater by dollar or right of way to displace landowners. Therefore, we can resolve a research question: how can the mechanisms of environmental review and public consultation explain the differences between the central project in Austin and its peers? The first step in understanding these mechanisms is understanding the atypical approach that TxDOT can take on environmental review processes.

The US National Environmental Policy Act (NEPA) requires FHWA to review the environmental process for highway projects, but TxDOT

Table 5.1: I-35 Capital Express Project environmental process

Segment	Project length in km (miles)	Construction cost	Hectares of right-of-way to be acquired (acres)	Draft environmental document date issued	Record of decision date	Days for environmental approval
North	18.5 (11)	$548 million	7 (17)	EA – April 19, 2021	December 17, 2021	243
Central	13 (8)	$4.5 billion	16.9 (41.7)	EIS – January 5, 2023	August 18, 2023	226
South	16 (10)	$388 million	5 (13)	EA – April 11, 2021	December 21, 2021	255

Note: EA=Environmental Assessment, EIS=Environmental Impact Statement.

is responsible for initiating, completing, and approving the agency's own environmental process, without federal review, called NEPA assignment. TxDOT's description of the process means that the environmental review process will conclude by a finding issued by TxDOT staff.

> The Surface Transportation Project Delivery Program (23 U.S. Code 327) allows the Secretary of Transportation to assign and a state to assume the Secretary's responsibilities under the National Environmental Policy Act and other environmental laws for highway projects. NEPA assignment streamlines the federal environmental review process by eliminating Federal Highway Administration project-specific review and approval, and provides a participating state specific review and approval authority. (TxDOT, 2019)

Since TxDOT maintains control of the planning, environmental, funding (with approval from the metropolitan planning organization), construction, and maintenance of the project, few alternatives exist to substantially change or stop the project. This legal mechanism leaves no other recourse for advocates to fight other than to sue.

A group of three plaintiffs, Rethink35, Texas Public Interest Research Group, and Environment Texas sued TxDOT in a federal district court, saying the agency 'improperly segmented the I-35 project into North, Central, and South Sections,' alleging that TxDOT sought to reduce the number of feasible alternatives to the project by having each segment go through a separate environmental process, since the North and South projects were approved through a concise Environmental Assessment, rather than the more in-depth Environmental Impact Assessment (Rethink35 et al, 2022, pp 22–620). After a year of litigation, the group dropped the lawsuit. Asked why the organizations stopped, Rethink35 Executive Director Adam Greenfield responded that 'for nonprofits like ours, we just don't have the capacity to fight multiple lawsuits at once. And while we haven't announced anything yet about our next steps legally, you can expect to hear an announcement from us in the coming months about subsequent legal action' (Saldana and Greenfield, 2023). Given a big highway with a long past and an uncertain future, a wider perspective can be helpful to think about how previous scholars find urban infrastructure is shaped through perception, power of social networks and socio-technical structures, and thinking and working together.

Resolving theories of transport agency narratives

I-35 is not the first case of transportation agencies deploying strategic narrative strategies, and there are many possible explanations behind the motivations, methods, and effects of communicative power for project development in democratic societies. A brief introduction to four concepts that engage how people work with technologies and social structures to impact their environments provides some clarity for possible mechanisms of the narratives deployed by transport agencies.

Urban obduracy is a notion that once constructed, features like transport infrastructure or large buildings become fixed in people's minds, becoming resistant to change even when alteration is rational through a given lens. Building on previous work on the social construction of technology (Bijker, 1995), obduracy is related to David Harvey's work on sunk investments—the idea that growth and maintenance of capital depends on urban infrastructure and a proximate local workforce. Through case study of urban redesign in the Netherlands, Anique Hommels also explained that 'socio-technical urban structures are always embedded in a broader network of rules, plans, policies, standards, institutions, and norms—a network into which they generally become even more solidity integrated, thus further adding to their obduracy' (Hommels, 2008, p 184). She posits three conceptions of urban obduracy, which are more symbiotic than competitive in explaining resistance to urban change. Frames of thinking or acting can help explain the perspectives of two or more social groups by how they perceive an urban technology as well-defined and mature technology, or 'closed' by those inside or outside the group. Embeddedness is a sociotechnical characteristic of the degree to which systems of planning, policies, or investments of money and constructed features are intertwined. Persistent traditions link local expectations of how planning is performed, with broader cultural traditions, and support continuity that could be historical or progressive. Hommels suggests that for urban obduracy to be overcome, cities must be unbuilt by actors' work through four strategies. First, they leverage specific social groups to overcome rigid thinking about a specific urban future. Second, they consider the interrelations of urban structures in a larger network as an approach to re-negotiate embedded elements. Third, they position persistent traditions as needing a radical change. Finally, they focus on changing the material environment as a key cause of urban obduracy, implying that a change in a technology such as a highway will tend to dismantle human expectations for the site. Together, this body of theory suggests that changes in the urban environment are most likely to succeed when pursued 'at a material level as well as at social, cultural, political, and economic levels' (Hommels, 2008, p 187). Hommels submits that urban obduracy may be less impactful in the United States, where more space exists for urban change without altering previous investments. However, this generalization could be less explanatory in highly-educated power centers like Austin, where pressures for preservation may run higher than in other cities. Obduracy may help explain resistance to change that underlies perspectives on the I-35 project.

Structural power depends on networks of power, but can stem from stable governmental mechanisms and capital, and may be most strong when both are in play. Theory-building on rationality and power suggests that when an evidence-based planning process begins to conflict with existing structures of power, including the operation of developers and construction firms working with elected officials, then rationality will yield to the power structures (Caro, 1975; Flyvbjerg, 1998). Not only will rational processes tend to fail when confronting power structures, but as Flyvbjerg proposes, 'power defines reality' (Flyvbjerg, 1998). This perspective is not unique to urban planning, nor its theorists. As John Forester pointed out, Foucault and Habermas both addressed systematically distorted communication and discourse (Forester, 2001), more currently known as misinformation or 'fake news.' Though Forester critiques Flyvbjerg's theory of rationality and power as over-generalizing in building propositions from what Flyvbjerg reported he knew about planning in Aalborg, I suggest that a lack of context or intentional nuance does not undercut the theory that 'power has a rationality that rationality does not know' (Flyvbjerg, 1998). In cases of transport planning, traffic forecasts provide a quantitative story about a future that has not happened, creating a narrative that carries structural power, because they are usually created by or for the governments proposing a change to the transport system. Review of 210 transport infrastructure projects built between 1969 and 1998 showed that about 40 percent of rail and 13 percent of road projects were off by more than 60 percent (Flyvbjerg et al, 2005). In an illustration of structural power in transit forecasting, Martin Wachs reflected on how power is used to re-define rationality (Wachs, 1990, p 144):

> I have interviewed public officials, consultants, and planners who have been involved in these transit planning cases, and I am absolutely convinced that the cost overruns and patronage overestimates were not the result of technical errors, honest mistakes, or inadequate methods. In case after case, planners, engineers, and economists have told me that they have had to 'revise' their forecasts many times because they failed to satisfy their superiors. The forecasts had to be 'cooked' in order to produce numbers which were dramatic enough to gain federal support for the projects whether or not they could be fully justified on technical grounds.

There are many studies seeking to build more robust travel models and a few more useful critiques, but some question whether the right tools are applied to the right problems in practice. Carole Voulgaris' interviews with transit forecasters showed that the requirements and context of a project impacts how they work in practice, and that 'planners can evaluate the likely trustworthiness of forecasts based on transparency, internal influence, and external influence' (Voulgaris, 2020). Taking an ontological perspective, Næss and Strand critique the use of model-based forecasts as inputs for analyzing costs and benefits of projects (Næss and Strand, 2012). They suggest forecasting 20–30 years in the future should follow a scenario-based approach because of the level of openness of many different factors impacting a given future; qualitative and simple calculations are appropriate at a tactical level, and micro-simulations are useful at a detailed operational level. Certainly, advancements in data and research to improve the practice of travel forecasting have been significant in recent years, and the US federal government has financially supported the 'Travel Model Improvement Program,' with a robust discussion forum and a toolbox full of reports and software beginning in 2008 (US Federal Highway Administration, 2023). However, these recent studies suggest that there may be more fundamental problems with the practice of model-based traffic forecasting.

The purpose of this connection between structural power and traffic forecasting is to propose possible explanations for strategic communication, not fully test it in the I-35 case. It is possible that traffic forecasts for I-35 could entirely be within bounds of practical accuracy for its uses, but if structural power were applied to strategically misinform communities or decisionmakers in Austin, it would not be unique.

Network power also engages topics of control and resistance through social communication that is mediated with technologies. Based on extensive empirical and theoretical studies, Manuel Castells proposes four types of power in the network society (Castells, 2011, p 773):

1. Networking power: the power of the actors and organizations included in the networks that constitute the core of the global network society over human collectives and individuals who are not included in these global networks.
2. Network power: the power resulting from the standards required to coordinate social interaction in the networks. In this case, power is exercised not by exclusion from the networks but by the imposition of the rules of inclusion.
3. Networked power: the power of social actors over other social actors in the network. The forms and processes of networked power are specific to each network.
4. Network-making power: the power to program specific networks according to the interests and values of the programmers, and the power to switch different networks following the strategic alliances between the dominant actors of various networks.

Each of these types of power contribute to three propositions of network power (Castells, 2013). First, power is multidimensional, and built around human interests and their networks, with a principal focus on influencing thought through mass communication media networks. Second, networks of power are linked through 'partnership and competition' that evolve through actors' engagement, but entire networks do not merge. Third, power of the state and its political system fundamentally structure the networking of power relations, both through coercive power (such as the police power which can involve violence) and persuasive power (such as use of media to guide thinking). From this perspective, control over communication networks dominate the balance of decision-making, even in democratic transport agencies. Public decisions reflect a struggle over power and counter-power that evolves networks toward goals of the groups and individual actors in those networks. These perspectives offer descriptive and theoretical explanations for urban planning systems, but they do not specify conditions that achieve goals that groups might agree lead toward working together toward solutions. Network power is one lens that could provide explanatory power for a *digital storytelling* planning mechanism in this chapter.

Collaborative rationality is a theoretical approach to planning that also centers networks, but seeks to adapt the system through authentic dialogue between the vested interests in a planning effort (Innes and Booher, 2018). Stemming from Jürgen Habermas's speech conditions for communicative action (Habermas, 1962, 1987) and John Forester's application of it to urban planning (Forester, 1980, 1988), Innes and Booher's conception of collaborative rationality depends on diversity, interdependence, and authentic dialogue (DIAD). First, the participants of collaborative planning must be sufficiently diverse, and there must be some interdependence between the groups. Participants then must engage in authentic dialogue, which follows from working towards reciprocity, relationships, learning, and creativity in the process. As a result, Innes and Booher seek adaptation of the system through identification of shared identities, meanings, finding new heuristics for working, and innovation in planning and policy. Without explicitly engaging with network power, collaborative rationality nonetheless relies on understanding and engaging the networks with a goal of finding common ground. Some may critique the approach as a fantasy given power relations (Allmendinger and Tewdwr-Jones, 2002; Murray, 2005), but evaluation shows that collaborative rationality is possible (Hollander, 2011). What some miss is that collaborative rationality is a normative theory in that it represents a desirable state, rather than a positive theory meant to merely explain existing conditions. Collaborative rationality may be helpful for analyzing what I call a *reconnecting communities* mechanism in the advocacy planning process for I-35. However, a critical realist might seek to separate which aspects of the planning process are structurally obdurate, and which are mechanisms that might be changeable.

Traffic forecasting as visioning

In the transportation planning office I worked in as an early-career planner around 2006, a co-worker who specialized in traffic modeling posted a sticker on a cubicle wall with a tongue-in-cheek maxim—models are precise to provide the illusion of accuracy. We were part of a regional transportation planning office, using travel demand models that use input data to 'forecast future travel demand based on current conditions, and future projections of household and employment characteristics' (Alexiadis et al, 2004, p 7).

I think my colleague was warning the visitors and bosses who arrived with questions about the future—those who ask what 'the model says' will happen if we build a road or change a context. Just because a traffic model can include a large number of variables and provide a volume-to-capacity ratio on an individual street to 20 decimal places does not mean it is right, or tell us how wrong either. But agency directors, mayors, or board chairs are not usually trained in modeling or statistics. Critical practitioners might conclude that transportation leaders are quite aware that modeling systems can be political, rather than statistical, tools. In *Confessions of a Recovering Engineer*, Chuck Marohn says it more bluntly. 'The goal of traffic modeling is not to be right; it is to create a plausible narrative as to why more construction is both needed and helpful' (Marohn, 2021, p 92).

Some analysts and agency heads might see the process differently. Guidance from the US Federal Highway Administration points to federal legislation that has 'reinforced the importance of traffic management and control of existing highway capacity' with 'an increased need to respond to recurring and nonrecurring congestion in a proactive fashion, and to predict and evaluate the outcome of various improvement plans without the inconvenience of a field experiment' (Alexiadis et al, 2004, p 3). In other words, staff can use models to manage transportation resources efficiently.

Travel demand models are only one broad category of tools, most often used to analyze traffic at regional geographies for strategic-level planning. Current state-of-the practice for major transportation projects also includes a later 'investment-grade' study that incorporates local economic conditions to give project financiers confidence of the construction and operation costs against agency revenue. Mesoscopic models focus on smaller areas and require much more information about local traffic conditions and driver behavior, and can 'simulate more details of individual vehicles' movements and produce more accurate simulation results' (Sun et al, 2020, p 764). Microscopic approaches extend these advantages further, most often to a single intersection or segment because they require a large amount of information and analysis time. Each study requires months of time and expertise from expensive consultants. Missed information can cost time that can kill projects. For instance, one additional month on a project costing

$4.9 billion could result in a loss of $16 million by inflation alone, using a conservative 4 percent annual rate. More analysis costs much more than consultant dollars.

This range of analysis tools demonstrates tradeoffs of microscopic detail and accuracy against the big-picture societal changes addressed by regional travel models, including demographic and regional economic fluctuations. Like many other major urban projects, I-35 in Austin is both a cause and a possible solution of regional and national societal changes impacting transportation, and a project with direct impacts to intersections with local streets, homes, and real people. The I-35 project is national and local, immediate and multi-generational. Getting it right is critical.

Recent traffic trends, as reported by TxDOT in their traffic count online maps (TxDOT, 2023d), showed bidirectional average annual daily traffic (AADT) on the freeway on the south side of downtown (station 227SP132) dropped less than 1 percent over the last decade, from 144,620 in 2012 to 143,425 in 2022. Just north of downtown near 41st Street (station 227H117), traffic rose imperceptibly, from 191,260 in 2012 to 191,475 in 2022, following an annual peak of 202,376 in 2018. So, if a traffic modeler were to hand-pick a period of the same station, say 2014–18 (11.2 percent growth), and assume a linear trend over the next 20 years, then traffic would balloon to over 315,000 vehicles daily by the year 2038.

In August 2011, the state published the 'My35' I-35 Corridor Advisory Committee Plan report to kick off a formal planning process created a narrative around traffic that was linked to population growth (TxDOT, 2011). The following excerpt shows how the document creates a narrative about traffic growth as linked to population growth, despite the disconnect seen in the traffic data.

> I-35 is the hub of transportation in Texas, serving varied users daily such as commuters, freight trucks, and business travelers. The diverse users of I-35 create substantial demand, with some sections of I-35 seeing over 200,000 vehicles a day. In fact, sections of I-35 made up 11 of the 100 Most Congested Roadways in Texas for 2010. With Texas' population growing over 20 percent in the last ten years, we can expect an even greater demand on the I-35 corridor.

The plan recommended widening I-35 'to a minimum eight-lane controlled access facility for a distance of approximately 124 miles [200 km]' with an estimated cost in 2010 of $2.7–3.85 billion, not including right-of-way purchases (TxDOT, 2011, p 124). The same plan also included a near-term, 112-mile regional passenger rail connecting San Antonio and Georgetown north of Austin, along a similar corridor to I-35, which would have provided an alternative for many passenger trips. In 2010, the Lone Star Rail District had begun the environmental clearance process that was expected to take up to 3 years, and estimated a total cost of $600 to $800 million. Despite the much lower cost of building rail, the region not only failed to fund the project, but decided to defund the rail district from existence in 2016 (Wear, 2016). If there is a passenger traffic problem in the region, then the region had decided that the freeway must also be the solution.

Part of the National Environmental Policy Act (NEPA) requirements for major projects like this is development of a draft environmental impact statement (EIS) that includes an evaluation of the project's purpose and need. TxDOT's draft Purpose and Need for the I-35 project did include travel demand, noting 'traffic congestion and operational deficiencies' (TxDOT, 2020, p 3). The document reported travel times from the year 2019, projected to the years 2025 and 2045 using traffic microsimulation models. Results showed pm-peak-hour northbound travel time increasing from 32 minutes to 131 minutes by the year 2025 and 223 minutes in 2045, resulting in 'mobility within the project limits in the near future will become unmanageable without substantive improvements' (TxDOT, 2020, p 5). Recalling previous research on the (mis)use of travel models, Næss and Strand showed the usefulness of microsimulation models for operational improvements—the opposite of long-term forecasting (Næss and Strand, 2012). TxDOT did not report specifics of how they expected traffic to continue growing—just that it would, wildly beyond any growth rates shown during Austin's years of rapid growth in population and employment.

Fortunately, the draft EIS does include more information about traffic— 3,575 pages published as 'Appendix H: Traffic Data' (TxDOT, 2023a). Professional engineer Matthew G. Best, representing the global firm HDR for TxDOT, authored a Traffic Projections and Methodology Memo showing that the historical average annual growth rate was 0.0 percent for the years 2003–18, though it increased to 0.4 percent for the last 10 of those years, but then follows traffic projections from the Capital Area Metropolitan Planning Organization (CAMPO), which assume an annual growth rate on the I-35 corridor of 1.49 percent between the years 2015 and 2045. (In full disclosure, I worked as a planner with CAMPO from 2006 to 2012, but was not involved directly in the Capital Express project.) The memo describes TxDOT's 'approval' of a 1.5 percent traffic growth rate from the base year of 2016, through the anticipated opening year in 2030, and the design year of 2050. After choosing to consider the annual trend in traffic from 2016 to 2019, Mr. Best's memo describes that the 'approved forecasts are not significantly out of line with current trends,' even though the 0 percent growth in traffic from 2003 to 2018 by their method would 'translate to an approximate increase of 15 percent traffic volumes between 2019 and 2030 and 45 percent between 2019 and 2050 for the central segment' (TxDOT, 2023a, p 8). Though the purpose and need started with a modeling narrative describing a 'microsimulation' implying a sophisticated rational process, we see that the actual traffic forecast was an 'approved' choice by the agency seeking approval for the project.

Of course, traffic modeling involves much more than a simple linear trend forecast for a few points along the freeway. Current state of the practice is a four-step modeling approach, including trip generation, trip distribution, mode choice, and traffic assignment, each of which are considered sub-models, where errors and biases can build upon each other (Ortúzar and Willumsen, 2011). Also in 'Appendix H: Traffic Data' is a 2018 memo from Mike Chaney, a consultant for Alliance Transportation Group, Inc., that includes a validation of the traffic demand model, that shows that the calibration across the entire county was 4 percent higher than the actual traffic counts, and 13 percent higher than the count at Lady Bird Lake (near the count station I previously noted on the south side of downtown). This validation is for the year 2010—the forecasters then applied the 'approved' 1.5 percent growth rate to generate trips in forecast years.

Traffic forecasts are also used beyond the direct storytelling of the number of vehicles on a highway or in a region—they are also used as input information to forecast other costs and benefits of a project. Official federal highway administration guidance shows that a primary purpose of these tools is to provide information for the Environmental Impact Statement (EIS) process (Alexiadis et al, 2004, p 4)—the legal evaluation of likely benefits and harms that determine whether a project receives federal funding and approval for construction. Outputs of the travel forecast become inputs for estimates of air quality (Appendix P), traffic noise (Appendix R), and greenhouse gas and climate change (Appendix V) and noise impacts for communities. Though not the focus of this chapter, the logic chain in this type of analysis is that 'traffic congestion results in lower average travel speed and increased idle time, which increases vehicle fuel usage. Therefore, the emissions benefits associated with less traffic congestion and improved travel speeds under Alternative 2 and Modified Alternative 3, as compared to the No Build Alternative' (TxDOT, 2023a, p 19 Appendix V). Following this logic, expanding a freeway may be construed as an environmental improvement, but this would only occur if for some reason people decided not to drive the newly-freed freeway—as if it would not induce new traffic demand. Given the cancellation of the regional rail effort, Texans are left with limited options.

Figure 5.3 integrates traffic forecasting as a method of visioning, in which the agency leaders both approved the traffic forecast that leads to seeking federal and state financing, and then also deploy vision and narrative through media discussed in the next section. Traffic consultants and agency employees are placed in an awkward ethical situation, because they follow the agency approved traffic forecast as a goal, and then create a narrative through both quantitative modeling and the report writing. A critical perspective—supported

Figure 5.3: Traffic forecasting as visioning mechanism

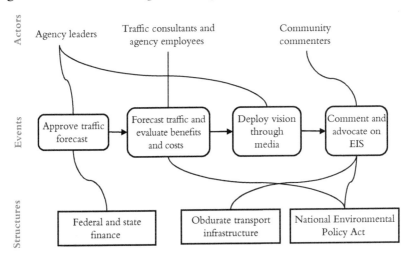

by previous research (Wachs, 1990; Flyvbjerg et al, 2005)—could suppose that meeting the agency-defined goals would also lead to continued support for the next agency project. Community members are left in the situation of having to comment on an environmental impact statement following this chain of logic, but lacking the ability to seriously critique the traffic forecast that was approved by the agency, and they never had access to the 'microsimulation' that led to the forecast in the first place. The case of I-35 shows how forecasting drives the purpose and need of a project but also evaluation of the benefits and costs in the environmental impact statement. Despite the consultant contracts, the late-night meetings, and over 2,500 public comments, the result is the same as the input—the 'approved' forecast drives the solution.

Traffic forecasting is a compelling type of visioning for a limited audience, but that audience arguably holds the greatest power—federal and state transportation leaders, and funding agencies. However, quantitative storytelling may not be the most compelling for public audiences, who agency leaders have learned are more likely to engage with compelling graphics and narratives.

Digital storytelling 'My35' and 'Our Future 35'

Digital storytelling techniques, such as the visual renderings, video presentations, and detailed schematics used by TxDOT in their 'My35' campaign, offer the advantage of precision and clarity. These tools allow for the visualization of complex infrastructure projects, thereby helping the public to better understand the scope, scale, and impact of proposed changes. Such vivid portrayals can foster greater public engagement and buy-in, and may even expedite the approval process. The high degree of realism also allows for a better assessment of the environmental and social impacts, facilitating more comprehensive public scrutiny. However, this approach is not without its disadvantages. The polished nature of digital renderings can sometimes give the impression that plans are more finalized than they may actually be, potentially limiting the scope for public input. High-quality digital media also require significant time and resources, and there's a risk that they may prioritize aesthetic appeal over functionality or feasibility.

In contrast, the city of Austin's 'Our Future 35' approach, which employed hand-sketching to convey design concepts, sends a different message. The hand-sketched plans suggest a level of openness and fluidity in the planning process, inviting public participation and comment. They implicitly communicate that the plans are not yet set in stone, thus encouraging more active engagement from community members who might feel that their input could lead to real changes. However, the downside of this approach is that it may lack the precision and detail that digital tools can provide. This can result in a less comprehensive understanding of the project's implications, thereby making it difficult for the public to fully grasp the potential impacts. It may also appear less professional or rigorous, which could undermine public trust in the planning process. Both approaches have merits and drawbacks, and the optimal strategy may involve a hybrid approach that capitalizes on the strengths of both digital and traditional methods of public communication.

Reconnecting communities

Local and national advocacy groups show disconnects between the state's planning for I-35 and local needs. The Frontier Group identifies the I-35 expansion as a 'boondoggle,' pointing out the widening to up to 20 lanes in some sections 'would displace up to 140 households and 70 commercial properties' (Horrox et al, 2022). TxDOT's Build Alternative 2 would have demolished a 70-unit affordable housing complex completed in 2019 – omitted as an oversight from using outdated aerial maps in their initial analysis (Bernier, 2022a).

Reconnect Austin contrasts the current state of affairs, with I-35 creating a wall between east and west downtown, and a redeveloped alternative showing the freeway buried, capped, and mixed-use redevelopment (Reconnect Austin, 2022).

Rethink35 is a local campaign pushing back against the I-35 expansion plan, re-route through-traffic to alternatives including SH-130 and US 183, and 'rethink I-35 through Austin as a boulevard' (Rethink35, 2023). They expect the expansion to worsen traffic in the city over the long term, consistent with this book's review of optimism bias and Braess's Paradox. Since the state had already built the toll road SH 130 as a bypass to central Austin traffic, they contend that the interstate highway is no longer needed.

Overall, they argue that moving through-traffic outside the city will improve Austin's livability. Through volunteer petitions, public protest, legal review, online media, and tangible items like yard signs, they aim to stop TxDOT's expansion plan for I-35 through Austin.

Though some may view this alternative as radical, the boulevard approach is historically the more traditional—and perhaps conservative—approach to street design (Jacobs et al, 2002). Before the common era, ancient Antioch and other middle eastern sites designed street networks around a central boulevard spine (De Giorgi, 2016). Boulevards with tree-lined separation of traffic and safe walking spaces were constructed in Paris as early as the 17th century, and then the concept was borrowed in US cities starting in the 19th century (Jacobs et al, 2002). Studies of traffic congestion and urban design impacts of boulevards and other street designs are widely available for review from other sources (for example, Dumbaugh and Rae, 2009; Institute of Transportation Engineers, 2010). Several key studies show how the nexus of this previous literature and planners' roles in the debate are critical for this chapter. Academic studies on urban design generally conclude that urban livability and design for individual motorized travel are incompatible goals, while recognizing that all current modes of transport are likely to have an important role in the future (Appleyard and Appleyard, 2021). This pushback against motorization as a dominant urban transport paradigm has not largely changed since the 1950s and 1960s, when Jane Jacobs and Lewis Mumford raised public alarms with public scholarship to bridge urban research and policy (Jacobs, 1961; Mumford, 1963). The livable streets movement identified more of the specifics of how these changes can happen, including empirical results and policy actions, resulting in decades of local and federal action (Appleyard and Appleyard, 2021). Stefan Gössling argues that cities need to redistribute space from cars for other modes to improve urban livability—that the physical changes are needed to support social changes, and that planners use 'communication strategies framing urban transport system change in ways that address driver concerns' (Gössling, 2020, p 447). Researchers and practitioners have developed new ways to democratize street visualizations like StreetMix (Streetmix, 2023), leverage tactical urbanism, embrace new funding approaches, and integrate land use planning to re-make streets as livable public spaces (Riggs, 2022).

TxDOT's environmental review authority granted through NEPA assignment is also a liability mechanism. Under a Memorandum of Understanding, the state of Texas can 'assume the Secretary's [of Transportation] responsibilities under the National Environmental Policy Act and other environmental laws for highway projects' (TxDOT, 2019). If this authority is not renewed by the Federal Highway Administration, it would expire December 19, 2024. As of fall 2022, TxDOT schedules the Environmental Impact Statement and Record of Decision to be complete by Summer 2023 (TxDOT, 2022).

Meanwhile, TexPIRG, Environment Texas, and Rethink35 filed a lawsuit on June 26, 2022, claiming that 'TxDOT is clearly violating the law' by separating the I-35 Capital Express projects within the Austin region into North, South, and Central projects to 'avoid the more rigorous, legally-required environmental review and public engagement of a single larger project' (Texas Public Interest Research Group, 2022).

Rethink35 protested the groundbreaking ceremony on November 15, 2022 for the I-35 Capital Express South project, which will add four managed lanes and frontage roads to the freeway south of Slaughter Lane. Local reporting showed the topic of induced demand was not debated by TxDOT. 'We're expected to double in population over the next 20 years or so, so the demand is here whether this project gets built or not,' the agency's District Engineer Tucker Ferguson said. 'We're being responsive to what's happening in our community and this is the right project to do at the right time' (Bernier, 2022b).

The last stage of the required public engagement process in the EIS is a public hearing, which TxDOT held in person at the Millenium Youth Entertainment Complex on February 9, 2023 for 2 hours between 5 and 7 pm. An online public hearing with a text commenting opportunity was open for comments from February 9 to March 7, 2023. Commenters provided 3,421 statements, mostly online in the form of a few sentences, and some sent in longer contributions as detailed letters. As a required part of the environmental process, TxDOT staff or consultants responded to each comment, often referring to a previously offered response, such as 'see comment #3.' In the following response edited for brevity, TxDOT addressed why several of the proposed alternatives were unacceptable.

> Several alternatives were provided by community stakeholder groups, including Reconnect Austin, Rethink35 and ULI Austin, for consideration in the design of the proposed project. To facilitate a fair and independent review of these community alternatives, TxDOT contracted the independent Texas A&M Transportation Institute (TTI) to review and evaluate the feasibility of these concepts. Following their evaluation, TTI concluded that none of the individual community alternatives would be viable as a build option on their own. Therefore, these concepts were not included for further, independent alternatives evaluation in the Environmental Impact Statement (EIS). Each community-proposed alternative had a variety of design concepts that would improve and enhance the alternatives that TxDOT is currently considering.

Despite describing their independence twice, the response misses the long, direct relationship between TxDOT and TTI. TTI's own self-authored history describes an arrangement beginning at the start of the Texas Highway Department in 1917, when they 'immediately began using the laboratory facilities of the Agricultural and Mechanical College of Texas. This marked the creation of a partnership that has continued to this day' (Texas A&M Transportation Institute, n.d., p 2). Of course, both agencies ultimately report to the same state governor. Many other university institutes, such as the Virgina Tech Transportation Institute or a private firm, could have provided more of an arm's length assessment of the alternatives with presumably less concern of lost revenue. The final design considered in the EIS did include concessions such as widened street crossings of the proposed expansion to I-35, along with bicycle and pedestrian infrastructure.

Although no additional alternatives analysis was shared with the public, TxDOT announced completion of the final EIS and record of decision on August 21, 2023. Speaking to reporters on the announcement, Rethink35 president Adam Greenfield responded that 'Transportation is the biggest source of carbon emissions locally. What are we doing? By widening a highway that's just going to worsen it. This is completely unacceptable' (Thompson, 2023). As of this writing, Rethink35 planned a press conference to announce next steps in their fight.

The prevailing narrative about urban freeway expansions often hinges on their detrimental environmental and social consequences. However, such a perspective may overlook the broader strategic imperatives of state and national-level trade and mobility that agencies like the Texas Department of Transportation grapple with. Expansions could, for instance, alleviate critical bottlenecks in transportation networks, facilitating a more efficient flow of goods and services that has far-reaching economic benefits. The potential for streamlined interstate commerce could enhance not just the competitiveness of Texas businesses but also catalyze economic growth at a national scale.

Contrary to the common notion that freeway expansions invariably result in increased traffic and pollution, there exist contexts where this is not the case. Integrated with advanced traffic management systems, well-designed expansions can contribute to smoother traffic flows, thereby potentially reducing harmful emissions caused by congested stop-and-go traffic. As electric vehicles become more prevalent, the environmental downsides of freeway use may diminish, challenging the notion that all freeway expansions are environmentally detrimental.

Critics often argue that freeway expansions disproportionately affect disadvantaged communities, but this doesn't have to be a foregone conclusion. Thoughtful urban planning and robust community engagement can guide projects in a way that minimizes social inequities. Such planning can include elements like green spaces and aesthetic features that actually improve the urban environment, offsetting potential negative social impacts. It's also worth acknowledging the significant role that freeways play during emergencies such as natural disasters, where the efficient mobilization of people and resources can literally be a matter of life and death.

Further, from a defense perspective, robust transportation networks are not merely a convenience but a strategic asset. The overarching state and national interest in ensuring rapid and efficient mobility often remains under-discussed but is an essential factor in evaluating the pros and cons of freeway expansion. Similarly, well-implemented freeway projects can be leveraged for broader urban development, attracting businesses and creating employment opportunities. When integrated into a multi-modal transport strategy that includes robust public transit options, freeway expansions can form part of a nuanced, multifaceted approach to tackling transport challenges.

Therefore, while it's vital to remain critical of the social and environmental impacts of freeway expansions, dismissing them outright may neglect the complex, multi-dimensional needs that such projects often strive to address. A balanced, empirically grounded evaluation might reveal that freeway expansions, when executed thoughtfully, can align with broader economic, social, and perhaps even environmental goals.

Contributions

This chapter demonstrated a critical realist approach to analyzing traffic forecasting in the Austin case of I-35, but there is little from this large-scale project that is not generalizable to many other major transport infrastructure projects. Leveraging several different theories about how the various actors in the case who worked within the events in which they were placed, we can see how structures both shaped the mechanisms that the actors were able to produce, and restrict what was capable. The traffic forecast that served the purpose in need of the environmental documentation for the entire project began with something that they call microsimulation, but we later found was actually driven by a decision that had no basis in modeling or analysis in the project. It was not rational but it was political. That decision became the basis for forecasting all of the benefits and costs and later scenario analysis involved in the project totaling billions of dollars. The structural power of transport finance systems within the United States instead of Texas along with the federal delegation of environmental responsibilities to the state, result in a lack of oversight across the process. The wolves watch the sheep.

Storytelling in this project is visual as well. Transport agencies and the advocates that counteracted their proposals deployed visual media strategically within meetings within traditional media and through social media to be able to shape and frame decisions by networks of power and how they would answer to the popular discourse. The city of Austin used visual storytelling through renderings of the cap and stitch proposals to shape support within the city and particularly the business community, to push text towards compromises that would lead to, in their perspective, a more livable city. More telling, is that TxDOT picked up on this perspective and gradually deployed visual renderings to show their perspective of how their vision meets the visual qualities that they expected the communities to accept. In this way, the agencies deployed network power within their own communities, and then merged with each other's power networks, to achieve their desired ends. Viewed from a lens of advocacy planning, which has a rich history in the US (Davidoff, 1965; Checkoway, 1994), visual storytelling and I-35 constitutes a neo-advocacy planning approach deployed by governments manipulating and collaborating with each other, rather than private sector advocates working against government agencies.

Finally, this chapter shows a rich opportunity to understand collaborative rationality, as deployed through the Reconnecting Communities concept. Advocacy groups, professional organizations including the urban land institute, in the city of Austin, begin to think and work together how to achieve common goals across their networks, deploying rich and thoughtful engagement to achieve their ends. However, TxDOT countered this approach by hiring the Texas A&M Transportation Institute to analyze and critique the traffic impacts of the proposals. In doing so, TxDOT turned collaborative rationality back into an instrumental form of rationality where a modeling tool can communicate what is right or best for a community in their minds. This chapter showed how actors in the Austin case deployed traffic forecasting, digital storytelling, and reconnecting communities to create a neo-advocacy framework for building power through competing transport truths.

If this case feels like a David and Goliath story because of the way local communities try to work against large, embedded structures in government and funding, the next chapter will illuminate even harsher discrepancies between the tiniest country on the continent of Africa with some of the richest countries in the world.

Box 5.1: I-35 in Austin takeaways for practice

- Transportation practitioners should reflect on professional ethics standards before, during, and after politically contentious projects that could coerce individual actions that can harm communities.
- Community advocates can leverage communication and media skills to increase access and knowledge about major government projects.
- Governments can advocate for and against other jurisdictions to follow local preferences, inverting traditional advocacy planning.
- Publics can address broader structures that endanger local democracy and autonomy by seeking and interrogating uncommonly known state and federal laws and policies, such as those enabling TxDOT to self-approve environmental reviews.

6

Development and Capital at the Banjul International Airport in The Gambia

Quite a distance from technological capitals, the Republic of The Gambia provides a complementary perspective that nonetheless is in its own moment of turmoil between the rules of power and development. This context shows how adding airport capacity is valuable for enabling growth and cultural connection in a region of West Africa with limited ground transport. The capital city of Banjul is a critical historical case, as a site of colonization and enslavement, and now a growing industry of diaspora tourism. As a nation colonized by the British empire, surrounded by the former French colony of Senegal, The Gambia is a modernizing nation seeking financial growth and autonomy. This chapter leverages Achille Mbembe's development of decolonial theory for both conceptual inspiration and critical lenses to review findings and meaning for the nation's prospects (Mbembe, 2021).

In The Gambia, the eagerness to accelerate the development of transport infrastructure often leads to a complex dance with foreign direct investment (FDI). External credit comprises 57.6 percent of the country's debt stock, or 48.9 percent of gross domestic product (GPD) (International Monetary Fund African Dept, 2021). Real GDP is forecasted to grow in the 5–6 percent range over the next few years, but another shock like the COVID pandemic could seriously endanger debt payments. This chapter delves into the particular investment of the Saudi Fund for Development's loan that enabled expansion of Banjul Airport—seizing a key opportunity to expand tourism, while deepening debts to foreign investors. This chapter addresses the degree that this type of foreign investment is a challenge to local development autonomy.

Banjul is both an economic lifeline for tourism in the nation today, and the historical core of the early transatlantic slave trade. This case study centers on expansion of Banjul Airport, including construction of a Very Very Important Person (VVIP) lounge through a loan by the Saudi Fund for Development, with a principal cost exceeding US$40 million. This study asks whether and how foreign direct investment is a challenge to local development autonomy (Davidson and Sahli, 2015), as shown in the expansion of Banjul Airport. Achille Mbembe's decolonialization scholarship (2021) suggests a possible conflict with local autonomy and foreign profiteering. Hence, Banjul may be considered a locus of neocolonialism (Okolo and Akwu, 2016), with deep irony considering its history. However, these investments do support new opportunities for local economic growth, though the balance of support vs. extraction is unknown. Case study methods include review of documents and official statistics with limited interviews of Gambian tourism professionals and students. Validity of tentative claims in this study were evaluated through member checking with local tourism practitioners. A critical realist perspective (Melia, 2020) informs depiction of the tourism infrastructure investment mechanism, showing the relationship between tourism entrepreneurship and infrastructure loans with the demographic structures of a youth population and foreign direct investment. Expansion of Banjul Airport through foreign loans can be construed as a neocolonial project, but that generalization obscures pragmatic goals for local growth. As The Gambia and other nations balance autonomy and development through managed foreign debt, targeted investments may provide key influx of capital for achieving decolonial goals.

This chapter shows evidence for foreign infrastructure investment that provides critical improvements, including expansion of Banjul Airport's runways, and in some cases, bridges and roadways. However, deepening debt for building a VVIP lounge may largely serve neocolonial interests, rather than supporting local entrepreneurial autonomy. A decolonial sustainable tourism would focus on the country's strength and its youth and its natural resources to build tourism entrepreneurship from a wide variety of sources rather than emphasis on foreign direct investment. However, there is a role for accepting critical foreign investments for infrastructure that supports local autonomy and entrepreneurism.

The crux of the tension often lies in the subtle erosion of local autonomy. As international investors bring in not just funds but also technical know-how, they tend to exert a growing influence over how the project unfolds, but may also spur domestic investment (Taylor, 2018). This influence isn't merely limited to construction blueprints or operational logistics; it can extend to determining user fees, service quality, and even labor sourcing. Local authorities may find themselves in a compromising position, with less agency over crucial decisions than they initially anticipated. While the project may technically be on Gambian soil, the strings controlling its operations might be pulled from a boardroom miles away.

Moreover, the terms of the investment agreement can cast a long shadow over local governance. Repayment conditions, for example, could mandate a certain revenue flow back to the investors, placing constraints on how local resources are allocated. In the event of economic downturns or fluctuating tourist numbers—scenarios not uncommon in emerging economies—these conditions could lead to strained public budgets and compromised local agendas. FDI offers the prospect of quick-build solutions, but have also been critiqued as facilitating 'plug-in urbanism' that favors external technological solutions to perceived local problems, and may lead to piecemeal changes to cities (Guma, Akallah and Odeo, 2023).

And yet, it would be reductive to cast FDI solely as a double-edged sword. The infusion of foreign capital and expertise can undeniably expedite projects that might otherwise remain on the drawing board for years. Moreover, the influx of tourists drawn by improved transport facilities can lead to increased local employment and ancillary business growth, creating a virtuous circle of economic development.

The complexity of tourism economies across the African continent vary widely according to long-term economic and political conditions, emigration, culture, and local histories. Banjul's context as a locus of modern tourism is tied with its history enduring colonialism and enslavement, with a complicated relationship to its commonwealth. The next section sets the stage of what makes Banjul such a special place to study FDI and autonomy of its urban development and tourism economy.

Roots and The Smiling Coast

The Banjul International Airport, also known as Yundum International, serves as a crucial gateway to the Republic of The Gambia, a relatively small yet historically complex nation on the West African coast. Not only does the airport facilitate international trade and connectivity, but it is also an integral part of the country's burgeoning tourism industry. Following a pre-pandemic peak of over 32,000 tourism arrivals in the month of November 2019, tourism has mostly recovered from shuttering in spring 2020 to 26,000 tourists arriving in November 2022 (Gambia Bureau of Statistics, 2023). Visitors come to experience The Gambia's cultural heritage, pristine beaches, and friendly community, summarized in a promotional slogan, 'The Smiling Coast.'

To fully appreciate the significance of Banjul's airport and The Gambia's tourist appeal, it is crucial to delve into the nation's historical context, particularly its colonial past rooted in the slave trade. The territory that is now The Gambia was an integral part of several West African empires, including the Mali and Songhai empires, before European colonization. Its geographical advantage—being a narrow strip of land on either side of the Gambia River—made it accessible for ships and thereby attractive to European powers, predominantly the British and French, who struggled for territorial control (Belda, 2006).

During the early stages of the transatlantic slave trade, the Gambia River was used as a channel to transport slaves from the interior regions of Africa to the Atlantic coast, where they were then shipped to European colonies in the Americas. The British established a stronghold in the form of Fort James, near what is now modern-day Banjul, serving as a collection point for enslaved persons. Although the slave trade was officially abolished in the British Empire by the early 19th century, its impacts were indelible, significantly altering the socio-cultural and economic landscape of The Gambia.

The nation's colonial history and the slave trade were pushed into global consciousness by Alex Haley's seminal book *Roots*, later adapted into a television miniseries. The book traces Haley's ancestry back to Kunta Kinte, a young man captured near the Gambian town of Juffure and sold into slavery. This narrative has made Juffure a place of pilgrimage for descendants of the African diaspora, enhancing The Gambia's cultural tourism while strengthening remembrances of the cultural and human costs of slavery.

After the abolition of slavery, British influence persisted, and The Gambia remained a British colony until it gained independence on February 18, 1965. The post-independence era saw the rule of Dawda Jawara, who steered the nation through initial stages of democratic governance. However, The Gambia was not immune to political instability, evidenced by the 1994 coup led by Yahya Jammeh. Jammeh's rule lasted for over two decades and was characterized by allegations of human rights abuses before he was eventually ousted in 2017.

In contemporary times, The Gambia is navigating a post-Jammeh landscape, focusing on legal reforms, improving human rights, and stabilizing its economy. The republic has a limited resource base due to its tiny overall size of 11,300 km^2 with an agricultural sector employing over two-thirds of the labor force and about 75 percent of total income (Food and Agriculture Organization of the United Nations, 2023). Primary crops include millet, rice, and groundnut (peanut), primarily dependent on seasonal rains for production. Climate change is a known risk to the agricultural economy and food availability for the country (Ceesay et al, 2021). Despite its small size and limited resources, the United Nations reports excellent progress by The Gambia on climate-related Sustainable Development Goals. Due to its position along the Gambia River and Atlantic Ocean, excellent fisheries and aquaculture opportunities exist, which the UN suggests can be developed further. Banjul is the country's largest metropolitan area, in addition to being home to a history of pre-colonial, colonial, and post-colonial urban planning. Recent research also shows problems in the city's administration regarding its unpredictability, disintegration, and lack of commitment to consistent and fair implementation of its urban planning efforts (Kolley et al, 2017). One of the central foci of The Gambia's economic strategy is to boost tourism, a sector that holds immense potential for employment and foreign exchange.

Tourism is so important to the country because it provides an opportunity for an influx of stable investment in local businesses. Foreign direct investment (FDI) has more than doubled since the year 2020 to 12.4 percent of Gambia's gross domestic product (World Bank, 2022). FDI can create opportunities to expand infrastructure and support the growing economy of The Gambia, but there is little to suggest that FDI will lead to greater economic autonomy. The opportunity and the burden of Gambia's sovereignty will be the responsibility of the present and next generations.

Youthful population is both a tremendous resource and a challenge for the country. Assessment of the country's skills gaps for youth show great opportunity for additional training in the tourism sector that can improve and diversify tourism products and services. These could include areas related to ecotourism and community-based tourism, sport activities, agritourism, and leveraging additional services associated with beach tourism (Republic of The Gambia, 2018). Yet, much of the country's youth are not ready to enter the workforce. Of the country's 2.4 million population, 39 percent is between 0 and 14 years old (CIA, 2023), which means that a high amount of investment is needed for children's needs including schooling. The youth dependency ratio (the youth population aged 0–14 per 100 people of working age—those aged 15–64) is 80.5 (CIA, 2023). This figure may not represent financial dependency directly, however, since some workers are moving abroad. The Gambia has lost between 2,000 and 4,000 people to migration every year since 1994 (World Bank, 2022). Personal remittances between expatriate workers and residents more than doubled between 2017 and 2021, comprising over 27 percent of the country's gross domestic product (World Bank, 2022). Remittances may help families avoid poverty and even build local entrepreneurship, but migration of workers may have social costs not recovered by wages.

The government has invested in infrastructural developments, of which The Banjul International Airport is a significant part. Given the airport's role as the main international entry and exit point, its functionality and efficiency are paramount for tourism to flourish. Banjul Airport, in this sense, can be seen as a metaphor for The Gambia itself. It stands at the crossroads of a complex history and an optimistic future. As tourists arrive at its terminals, they are not merely entering a destination renowned for its beaches and biodiversity; they are also stepping into a country that has endured the multifaceted legacies of empire, enslavement, and authoritarianism. As The Gambia leans into its tourism identity of 'The Smiling Coast,' it does so with a deep awareness of its past and a hopeful eye towards a more prosperous, inclusive future. Thus, the airport serves as a critical juncture that connects

The Gambia's historical roots with its contemporary ambitions, encapsulating its journey from a dark colonial past to a future illuminated by the smiles of its people and the beauty of its land.

Climate for travel and tourism

In recent years, The Gambia has undertaken a variety of strategic initiatives aimed at promoting travel and tourism, recognizing the sector as a cornerstone for economic development and foreign exchange earnings. Given the multidimensional appeal of the country, these endeavors involve a mix of policy reforms, public–private partnerships, infrastructural development, and international collaborations.

The Gambia has also sought to diversify its tourism offerings beyond traditional 'sun, sea, and sand' attractions shown in Figure 6.1. Ecotourism is one such focus, with protected reserves such as the River Gambia National Park and the Tanji Bird Reserve offering immersive experiences into The Gambia's unique biodiversity. Efforts are underway to maintain these environments sustainably while making them accessible for educational and recreational tourism. Cultural tourism leveraged the global recognition brought about by Alex Haley's book *Roots* and its subsequent adaptations. Heritage sites like Juffure and Kunta Kinteh Island have been better preserved and are being promoted as key points in the transatlantic slave trade's historical memory. This appeals to diasporic communities and history enthusiasts,

Figure 6.1: Atlantic Ocean beachfront in The Gambia

Source: Dick Knight, flickr 2018

adding a poignant layer to The Gambia's tourism landscape. Survey research of tourists in The Gambia also suggests that additional site and infrastructure development in rural areas could benefit local economies and reduce leakage to outside firms (Rid et al, 2014). The government has introduced favorable visa policies and incentives to encourage foreign investment in the tourism sector. These include tax breaks and eased regulatory hurdles for entrepreneurs investing in hospitality and travel-related services. Collaborations with international travel agencies, participation in global tourism expositions, and partnerships with influencers and travel bloggers aim to boost the country's profile as a must-visit destination. A robust digital marketing campaign has been another lever in The Gambia's tourism promotional strategy. Through the effective use of social media platforms, The Gambia Tourism Board aims to reach a broader and younger audience. Vivid visual storytelling, featuring the country's picturesque landscapes and vibrant cultural events, is employed to captivate potential tourists. These efforts are largely internally funded, but coordination with private entities and international funding are needed for projects that require a greater capital investment.

Public–private partnerships are being fostered to support growth in tourism, particularly in hotel and resort construction. Some of these collaborations involve training programs aimed at building the capacity of local stakeholders in the tourism value chain—from hotel management to tour guides—to meet international standards. The aim is to create a holistic experience that complements the natural and cultural attractions with high-quality service. However, interviews with University of The Gambia tourism students, most of whom are also employed in the industry, showed that these partnerships tend to financially favor the corporations' home offices, often located in England or other sites outside The Gambia. Some newer projects include community engagement initiatives to ensure that the benefits of tourism filter down to local populations, which can also foster a sense of ownership and responsibility towards sustainable tourism practices. By integrating local crafts, cuisine, and traditional performances into the tourism experience, not only is a unique product offered to tourists, but economic gains could also be more evenly distributed. Several students I interviewed also mentioned needs for expanding transportation infrastructure like roads and airports. Transportation statistics show gains in paving dirt roads and other key initiatives, but major new projects often require international investment.

The Gambia has also worked to expand transportation support for international tourism and economic development through external funding sources. External investments have been a key tool for infrastructure development, including Banjul Airport. The Saudi Fund for Development provided a loan of over US$31 million for capacity improvements to the airport, in addition to a US$10.5 million loan to build a VVIP lounge to 'host official delegations and international conferences' (Saudi Fund for Development, 2022). Gambia Vice President Dr Isatou Touray and the CEO of the Saudi Fund for Development, Sultan bin Abdulrahman Al-Marshad, inaugurated the project to lay the foundation stone for the VVIP lounge with members of the press present in November 2021. The debt to SFD is on top of other loans for the same airport, such as an US$8 million loan in 2009 from the OPEC Fund, to pay for the second phase of the Banjul Airport Rehabilitation Project, with the total project cost estimated at US$34.9 million (OPEC Fund, 2023). As the tiny country's debt accumulates for these projects, the role of FDI may strain recent gains in real or perceived electoral fairness and transparency. Other key infrastructure loans from foreign investors include a US$20 million agreement with the OPEC Fund for International Development (OFID) for a 22 km-long expansion of the Bertil-Harding Highway (Emirates News Agency, 2021). Emirates News Agency also describes OPEC Fund commitments of 'close to $128 million supporting transportation, education, energy and multi-sectoral projects,' to the tiny nation.

The Gambia is not the only country experiencing these development finance pressures, and decolonial perspectives seek to empower local systems to remove legacies of control. Critic of colonialism Achille Mbembe contextualizes this international experience with a warning to look out for the precarity imposed by extractive relationships, which may prove most impactful in moments of turmoil.

> There is no accident without some form of collision, or even collusion. Three such instances of collision and collusion are reshaping the [African] continent. There is, first of all, collision and collusion that occur when privatization has to be carried out in an environment structurally characterized by privation, dispossession, and predation. A second type of collision and collusion occurs when extraction goes hand in hand with abstraction in a process of mutual constitution. After all, the places where capital is most prosperous on the continent today are extractive enclaves, some of which are totally disconnected from the hinterland, in some nowhere that is accountable to nobody except to petro-capital. The third instance of collision and collusion comes in the form of a structural convergence of massive social upheavals, profiteering, and war. Here, in order to create situations of maximum profit, capital and power must manufacture disasters and feed off disasters and situations of extremity that then allow for novel forms of governmentality. (Mbembe, 2021, p 30)

Mbembe's perspective suggests that following the investment trail may help identify areas of caution, if such problems exist. Postcolonial critical realist theory suggests that subaltern lived experiences make visible the reality of racialized power struggles, and that this coloniality is driven by power that is resistant to change and often difficult to identify (Tinsley, 2021). A growing number of scholars question the role of foreign direct investment in Africa, particularly when support could be less than altruistic, but could provide investors footholds in growing economies and access to African resources, which may have the same impacts as neocolonialism (Okolo and Akwu, 2016). The opposite of foreign direct investment in countries experiencing financial hardships, however, could be interpreted as ignoring opportunities to help our brothers and sisters. One measure of success of FDI is the degree that it stimulates local investments for diversification and sustainability of African economies (Taylor, 2018). Scholars of China's investments under the Belt and Road Initiative (BRI)—designed to bring a new era of Silk Road trade with overland and maritime partners—show the potential for foreign investment to realize greater gains through 'influx of Chinese economic firms and companies in these emerging markets' (Meyer, 2019, p 130). The implications of foreign aid to The Gambia and similar countries include likely short-term economic development gains, balanced by risks of domestic sovereignty over time—depending on the county's ability to repay loans and maintain diplomatic relations. Delving into an example of investment meant to facilitate economic development can provide a glimpse of some of the challenges and opportunities for local economic growth.

Who pays? Who benefits?

The Republic of The Gambia has a single paved airport, Banjul International, shown in Figure 6.2, which makes this infrastructure the critical path for international tourism. The airport has been effective for many years, but some viewed its total capacity as limiting growth, and that it needed to cater to a demanding clientele to leverage additional interests and investments. The Saudi Fund for Development's decision to support these expansions produces both direct support for key infrastructure, and an increase in indebtedness for a very small economy.

Through a press release about the project, Sultan bin Abdul Rahman Al-Marshad said, 'This is an important milestone in the growth and prosperity of The Gambia. The expansion of Banjul International Airport is an extension of the ongoing support provided by the Kingdom of Saudi Arabia to the Republic of The Gambia, which includes 14 development loans and five grants with a total value of US$215 million across transport, education, water, and economic development' (Saudi Fund for Development, 2022).

Is The Gambia continuing to re-live colonialism through financial indebtedness? In a critical perspective, Stefano Liberti explains Saudi investment policy through the words of King Abdullah, 'This is an old

Figure 6.2: The Banjul International Airport is a key hub for the country's tourism

Source: Salvador Aznar, Shutterstock 2017

phenomenon. The Gulf States are only doing now what the Europeans have done for years' (Liberti, 2013, p 54). He argues that the Persian Gulf nations' investment in Africa are driven by access to agricultural land. Given the lack of arable property in the Saudi desert, one can imagine the potential for risk by The Gambia's indebtedness to Saudis. The issue of foreign investment is not constrained to individual transportation or tourism projects. Critical research suggests that the effectiveness of the support for the country is dependent on the strength of the state. Detailed case studies of attempts for urban planning in The Gambia suggest that indebtedness may suppress efforts to conduct comprehensive urban planning for development (McGrath, 1989).

Hotel construction is also critical for growing tourism in The Gambia. A study of the Gambian hotel sector showed that foreign direct investment largely supported the larger and more expensive hotels which also tended to hire larger numbers of staff who are paid greater wages and receive more training (Davidson and Sahli, 2015). However, employment was more likely seasonal, and they tended to employ fewer women. These findings suggest that there is an important role for FDI in tourism infrastructure but that dependence of FDI could exacerbate inequalities and lead the leakage in local tourism revenue.

Analysis of overall infrastructure needs by the International Monetary Fund shows that active policies to mobilize domestic revenue, improve the efficiency of existing government spending, and continue to attract additional private investment, could cover most of the infrastructure gaps through the year 2030 (International Monetary Fund African Dept, 2021). A dynamic financing framework that leverages government revenue with both public and private resources suggests that improvements in human capital including health and education in infrastructure such as roads, water, and power lead to increases in gross domestic product. That increase then symbiotically increases government revenue, improving the cycle of development. However, the International Monetary Fund concludes that all these efforts are still unlikely to close its infrastructure gap by the year 2030, finding that additional grants are needed totaling 1.8 percent of GDP per year, if all of these policies are implemented, and more if only portions of these policies are implemented.

These potential risks to domestic sovereignty must be considered from a practical perspective from those who stand to gain. The Gambia would not be consulting with outside investment opportunities if they didn't have a direct need or an application for the support. Additionally, broad-based support by the World Bank and others not representing a single interest continues to support development in the country. The World Bank's long time support for tourism in Africa focuses on policy reform building capacity locally, linking to private sector needs, and ensuring tourism products are competitive in the global marketplace (World Bank, 2011). If the Gambian proverb, 'giant silk cotton trees grow out of very tiny seeds' (Belda, 2006, p 143) is believed, some of these key projects supported by foreign interests could enable great returns for local communities and their descendants.

On May 4 and 5, 2024, The Gambia hosted the 15th Islamic Summit of Heads of State and Governments of the Organisation of Islamic Cooperation (OIC), a key opportunity to showcase recent developments, including expansion of the airport runway and VVIP lounge. As confirmed through local tourism professional and former University of The Gambia student Bubacarr Camera, timely completion of the VVIP lounge was a key priority of the OIC Secretariat. Mr Camera confirmed to me through text messaging three strategic benefits of the VVIP lounge:

1. supporting extended tourism year-round;
2. improving tourism infrastructure that could lead to a change in The Gambia's tourism offerings; and
3. complementing the new conference center as a go-to destination for international conferences and facilities, and improving The Gambia's competitive advantage as a service destination for both regional and international airlines.

Through extensive coordination, the VVIP lounge and its facilities were completed in time for the summit, yet many of the thousands of visitors and delegates likely could not land at The Banjul International Airport, as described by Sheriff Bojang Jnr of The Africa Report. The Yoff Airport in Dakar was able to provide additional facilities needed by visitors. This limitation may have mitigated some of the benefits of such a major event, but The Gambia nonetheless successfully hosted it, including delegates of many of the loaning agencies represented among the attendees.

If we can consider Gambian tourism workers as the central focus of action to support sustainable tourism, we also have to consider the roles of expatriate workers and foreign interests in the flow of capital. As shown in Figure 6.3, Gambian tourism is precariously dependent on the rules of remittances and infrastructure development of the FDI that it is largely supported by. The interaction between tourism entrepreneurship and infrastructure loans can be symbiotic, but it can also be extractive. This study shows no evidence of wrongdoing by either Gambian authorities or Saudi investment interests. However, Achille Mbembe's warning call shows that there is good reason to be concerned about the prospect of privatization of Gambian resources that could lead to disempowerment of local interests and control over the growing tourism industry. Converging risks of climate change, regional instability, and unknown future factors, a concerted effort to support a decolonial sustainable tourism for The Gambia is a laudable goal. One of those unknown future factors might be the role of global consumption of minerals from central Africa in the prospect of Gambia's river serving as an important outlet for a new generation of exported products.

Figure 6.3: Tourism infrastructure investment mechanism

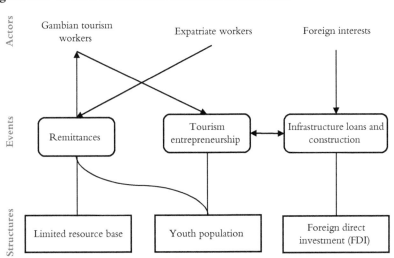

Sustaining cultures

Though significant, Saudi Arabia may not be the most threatening external power to The Gambia and other African nations. 'China is now the worlds' largest consumer of Africa's copper, tin, zinc, platinum, and iron ore, and a large consumer of Africa's petroleum, aluminum, lead, nickel, and gold' (Mbembe, 2021, p 36). The Gambia does not export these materials directly, but the Gambia River and port may be a critical component of the international export of minerals from Saharan and sub-Saharan nations. International interest in The Gambia may be most powerful by leveraging the nation's transport infrastructure, including its river—the same vessel of its original colonization. The nation's next steps with its partners may be critical for the role of its democratic determination of the future.

In the context of Achille Mbembe's decolonial theories, the issue of high-income countries offering loans for infrastructure to smaller African nations raises intricate questions about power, sovereignty, and cultural agency. Mbembe's postcolonialism elucidates the often unspoken conditions and constraints under which African nations navigate their relationships with global powers.

Firstly, it's important to acknowledge the historical backdrop: many African nations have a history of colonial exploitation, where not only were natural resources extracted, but cultural and societal structures were systematically undermined. In this setting, loans from high-income countries can act as a contemporary form of neocolonialism, perpetuating dependency and limiting sovereignty. While these loans are ostensibly for development, they often come with stringent conditions that can result in debt traps and policy prescriptions that do not necessarily align with the social and cultural fabrics of these nations. Sustaining cultures in this context is not merely a matter of preserving traditions; it's an act of political resistance and a reclamation of agency. According to Mbembe, the postcolony is a space of hybridity, where the legacies of colonialism interact with traditional and modern forms of governance and culture. However, the postcolony is not just a passive recipient of external influences but is capable of actively shaping its own destiny. Preserving and nurturing local cultures can act as a form of resistance against the monocultural global capitalist paradigms often imposed by high-income countries. This is consistent with Mbembe's view that the postcolony must engage in a form of 'outward looking,' actively participating in global discourses, but without erasing its own multiplicities and complexities. Furthermore, the act of sustaining cultures serves as a counter-narrative to the often reductionist portrayal of African nations as merely 'underdeveloped' or 'corrupt,' providing a more nuanced understanding of their complexities. This enables a form of governance that is more attuned to local needs, traditions, and aspirations, rather than one dictated by external economic metrics or cultural values. Lastly, by sustaining cultures, African nations can engage in what Mbembe would describe as a kind of 'world-making,' where the nation is an active participant in the global conversation, not just a subject of global forces. This agency allows for a more equitable dialogue between nations and can serve as a platform for the kind of multiplicity and pluralism that Mbembe advocates for. Thus, from a decolonial perspective informed by Mbembe's work, sustaining cultures is integral in retaining agency, autonomy, and a complex sense of identity when interacting with high-income countries and their financial instruments.

Critiques of decolonial thought as it pertains to transportation planning for economic development often focus on the practical, ideological, and epistemological dimensions of this theoretical approach. One common critique pertains to the tension between idealism and pragmatism. Decolonial thought often calls for radical shifts in planning paradigms, demanding local agency and cultural preservation. However, the economic imperatives driving transportation infrastructure—such as efficiency, cost-effectiveness, and integration into global supply chains—can sometimes be at odds with these ideals. Critics argue that in the quest for decolonization, there's a risk of downplaying or sidelining the very real economic challenges and needs that such infrastructure projects are designed to address. A decolonial approach that is too prescriptive might constrain the pragmatic flexibility needed for economic development.

Another critique revolves around the applicability and universalization of decolonial concepts. While decolonial thought provides invaluable critiques of the colonial underpinnings that often shape transportation planning, critics argue that its lens may not be universally applicable or may inadvertently homogenize experiences across different regions and communities. Decolonial theories often emerge from specific historical and cultural contexts, and their application to diverse settings can risk a form of epistemological colonization, where one theory or framework is considered universally valid. This can be particularly problematic in multi-ethnic or pluralistic societies, where the quest for a singular, 'decolonized' approach might overlook intra-national complexities and heterogeneities.

Lastly, some critics point to a perceived tension between the focus on cultural preservation in decolonial thought and the dynamics of change and modernization that often accompany economic development. The decolonial emphasis on sustaining traditional practices and local knowledge might come across as resistant to innovation or technological advancement. In the realm of transportation planning, where advances in technology (such as green energy solutions, smart urban planning, and digital networking) are increasingly integral to sustainable economic development, critics question whether decolonial frameworks can adequately reconcile the past's preservation with the imperatives of future-oriented development.

Thus, while decolonial thought offers critical insights into the power dynamics and historical legacies shaping transportation planning, it is not without its critics. These critiques serve as important counterpoints that enrich the ongoing dialogue around how to enact equitable, sustainable, and culturally sensitive economic development through transportation planning.

Contributions

This chapter showed how the particular structures of The Gambia create a context where sustainable growth in tourism is likely, but the role of FDI on indebtedness and independence is uncertain. This critical realist case study goes deeper than a simple analysis of transactions or cursory review of interviews, to share the linkages between financial power structures that have an outsized role in the context of nations with lower resource availability. The history and role in global colonialism does not have to dictate its future. A decolonial sustainable tourism would focus on the country's strength and its youth and natural resources to build tourism entrepreneurship from a wide variety of sources, rather than emphasis on foreign direct investment. The country's high adoption of smartphone access and nearly ubiquitous use of English as a lingua franca positions it well to accomplish these goals in an era of crowdfunding and microloans. However, growth in the tax base may not be adequate to be able to replace that capital needed to be able to build the infrastructure necessary to support rapid growth in the tourism sector. Indicative of its small stature and a rapidly developing continent, neocolonial foreign powers may leverage loans and infrastructure projects to target The Gambia's critical role in Africa's natural resources while the global economy pivots toward electrification and automation. Judicious evaluation of foreign investments can support a decolonial pathway toward Gambian self-determination.

Box 6.1: Banjul Airport takeaways for practice

- Developing countries are subject to foreign investment that may counter long-term autonomy.
- Foreign loans for the expansions of Banjul Airport and other key infrastructure may support tourism growth, but also exert pressures that hinder postcolonial independence.
- Case study analysis shows little evidence that the VVIPs lounge funded by the Saudi Fund for Development has fostered local economic autonomy to date.

7

Triangulating Transport Knowledge

The previous chapters have explored how people can view the same transport phenomena and come away with varying, even oppositional decisions about their origins, impact on society, and ways to improve outcomes. Reflecting on the case studies, this chapter first contrasts issues in sequencing data and findings, recognizing that prioritizing datasets has implications on later analysis and possibly, conclusions. Mixed data can be integrated at different levels, as well. A first approach for researchers may prioritize the tradition with which the researcher is most familiar. However, a fully integrated approach of simultaneous quantitative-qualitative data collection and analysis may reveal connections between each strand of data, enabling real-time adjustments that better reflect realities. This chapter includes a typology of mixed methods research designs, shown in Figure 7.1, that will aid alignment of knowledge to action. As an example of an emerging approach, I focus on how crowdsourcing—a digital approach to gather knowledge from a large group—can support transport planning in a co-productive approach. In co-production, local participants and planners are considered equals in the production of knowledge, development of solutions, and implementation—when the toolsets and power dynamics are shared. This approach can nonetheless result in conflicting answers to the same problems, which is why this approach for triangulating knowledge may be so powerful. Following recent guidance on integrating mixed methods (Creamer, 2018), this chapter shows how researchers can construct meta-inferences from divergent approaches to transport problems.

Sequencing transport truths

In the realm of transport research, understanding real transport phenomena demands a multi-layered approach that effectively sequences data analysis. Sequencing of data and findings significantly impacts the inferences drawn. Prioritizing different datasets, changing the order of quantitative and

Figure 7.1: Simplified triangulation of mixed-method truths with ethical filter and action

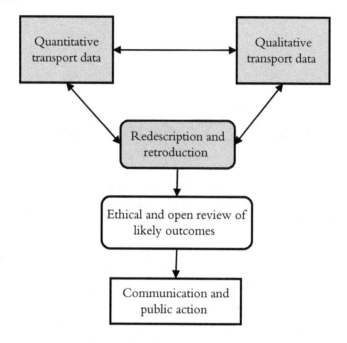

qualitative data analysis, and considering what time period the data represents, all impact the process and outcomes of analysis.

Regarding which data to analyze first, analysts could consider both their own understanding and the relationship between the data and research questions. Initially, professionals may opt to prioritize the data sets and analytical methods they are most familiar with. Known as familiarity-based sequencing, this offers a baseline understanding and is a practical approach, especially for early-career researchers. Alternately, relevance-based sequencing: a more strategic approach may involve prioritizing datasets by their relevance to the core research questions. This ensures that the most impactful data are analyzed first, setting the tone for subsequent data analysis. Chapter 6 reviews some basic quantitative measures about the tourism industry to help frame understanding about the context in The Gambia before going more deeply into qualitative analysis leading to understanding of tourism infrastructure mechanism.

How researchers integrate numerical and non-numerical data is also key. Sequential mixed-methods integration starts with either qualitative or quantitative data as a point of departure. The insights derived from the initial analysis can guide the subsequent analysis, whether it be qualitative or quantitative, in a confirmatory manner. A more advanced approach is to concurrently analyze qualitative and quantitative data, aimed at drawing meta-inferences (Creamer, 2018). This enables real-time adjustments in the analytical framework, which may better reflect the complex realities of transport phenomena.

The time represented by the dataset, or how the researcher can break apart a larger dataset into temporal segments, allows different understanding of the phenomena. A cross-sectional approach offers a snapshot, while a longitudinal approach can reveal mechanisms and events that unfold over time (Hansson et al, 2011; Chen et al, 2017). In Chapter 5, time plays a key role in how the environmental process differs between similar projects. Analyzing the different segments of the same freeway corridor gives an unexpected result where the more complex project took less time to approve environmental documents. If a cross-sectional approach had been taken, only looking at the key project of interest—the Central segment—then it is quite possible that this key distinction would have been missed.

Challenges in full integration of transport studies

Analyzing qualitative and quantitative data simultaneously in transport studies is an intricate endeavor that encompasses a range of challenges. Epistemologically, the two types of data often arise from differing paradigms—quantitative data tends to stem from a positivist viewpoint focusing on empirical observations, while qualitative data often aligns with interpretive frameworks that emphasize context and meaning. These foundational differences present hurdles in conceptual alignment, as the narrative, context-specific nature of qualitative data often does not easily dovetail with the standardized variables of quantitative research.

Methodologically, the integration of these disparate data types presents its own set of complexities. Each has its own analytical tools, complicating the synthesis of results. While quantitative data is usually subjected to statistical rigor to establish its validity and reliability, qualitative data might be validated through methods like triangulation or member checks, making the simultaneous validation of mixed data a nuanced process. The scale and granularity of the data can also differ significantly, as qualitative research often focuses on depth, possibly in smaller sample sizes, while quantitative methods aim for breadth and generalizability (Hennink and Kaiser, 2021). Practically speaking, the resource intensity required for effective mixed-methods research is often high, demanding significant investments of time, finances, and expertise. The logistics of simultaneously collecting diverse types of data further complicate matters. Additionally, the sheer volume of data that could be collected might result in analytical overload, raising issues in data management (Bogdan and Bilken, 2003).

On the ethical and social front, informed consent processes may differ for each type of data, and when involving local participants in a co-productive approach, balancing power dynamics becomes an additional challenge (Mitlin, 2008). Finally, one must be prepared to resolve conflicting findings that arise when diverse types of data provide divergent answers to the same research questions. Despite these complexities, the richness and depth that can be achieved through a well-executed mixed-methods approach make it an invaluable strategy for understanding the intricate realities of transport phenomena.

Classifying mixed-methods designs for transport research and practice

Transport research is a multidisciplinary field that often benefits from employing mixed-methods approaches to generate nuanced insights. Several categories can delineate different types of transport research approaches that incorporate mixed methods.

In explanatory sequential designs, researchers start with quantitative data collection and analysis. Subsequently, qualitative methods are employed to help explain or interpret those initial quantitative results. This is particularly useful when the quantitative results require contextual elaboration or when unexpected patterns emerge that can't be understood through numerical data alone.

Exploratory sequential designs start with qualitative data collection, followed by quantitative methods. Researchers employing this design might begin with in-depth interviews or focus groups to identify variables or construct instruments, which are then tested quantitatively in a broader context. This approach is useful when studying newly emerging issues where established measures and instruments may not yet exist.

Convergent designs involve simultaneous collection of qualitative and quantitative data, but separate analysis. After the separate analyses, the data are compared or related to construct a comprehensive understanding of the research question. This approach is useful for studies aiming for validation through data triangulation and can help in understanding complex transport phenomena through multiple lenses.

Embedded designs allow one form of data to support the other, essentially embedding one within the other's analysis. For instance, qualitative data may be used to aid in the interpretation of the findings derived from a primarily quantitative research design, or vice versa. This design is beneficial when researchers have a primary method but recognize that an auxiliary method could provide added value.

Transformative designs focus is on addressing social justice or policy issues, and the choice between qualitative and quantitative methods is governed by the research question. The data may be collected simultaneously or sequentially, but the emphasis is on using the data in a complementary manner to advocate for change. This is particularly useful for transport studies focusing on topics like equity in public transit access or environmental justice. This emancipatory research design can leverage critical realist perspectives on both the nature of reality, and an ethical obligation to enact change based on that knowledge (Banai, 1995; Tinsley, 2021). Enacting change is often outside the scope of research, however, but there are approaches for those that are willing to give over study outcomes.

Participatory or community-based designs can incorporate elements of co-production, where stakeholders or community members actively participate in the research process. Qualitative and quantitative methods can be employed iteratively and adaptively based on community input. These designs are valuable in studies focusing on local transportation needs, urban planning, and sustainability (Cooper, 2007; Golub et al, 2018).

By understanding the particular affordances and limitations of these categories of mixed-methods research approaches, scholars can more strategically align their research designs with their questions, thereby generating insights that are both empirically robust and rich in contextual nuance.

Co-producing knowledge with crowdsourcing

One example of co-productive crowdsourcing is a new platform for aggregating the route preferences of bicyclists called Ride Report (Knock Software, 2017), which can be used as an example of all five of Watson's distinctions of co-productive planning (Griffin, 2019). Ride Report was a smartphone-based crowdsourcing platform that automatically recorded GPS tracks of bicycle rides, that were detected using a combination of accelerometer data with speed detected through GPS. When the app detected the end of a trip, it automatically came up with a question to the user about the quality of that route. On the back end, Ride Report aggregated those trips across each roadway segment in a community, yielding both average rating values and bicycle traffic volumes—information co-produced with the system users that could inform city planning, but also advocacy to push government further with actionable information on bicycle routing.

This system reverses the flow of traditional knowledge in transportation, such as motorized level-of-service models that use a priori standards imported from expert knowledge to a bottom-up rating system that is constructed by participants in the context of their actual routes. Planners can use the resulting aggregated map of route preferences for future improvements, but it also provides a real-time bicycle map to inform users' route choices. Traditionally, engineers and planners' information is a source of power (Innes, 1998), which this method provides to its users, supporting advocacy supported by data. This type of crowdsourcing is centered on GPS data, and a comfort rating of routes, rather than discussion—users see the result of their contributions, and can learn how their own experience of the city is situated with others'. Finally, automation of the platform supports scaling beyond the local level, with the numbers of participants and sufficient server space the only limits to the scaling of the system.

Whereas communicative and collaborative traditions are rooted in well-developed, democratic societies (Healey, 2003), co-production's roots are from the global South, supporting planning at varying levels of cooperation with state-sanctioned planning (Watson, 2014). Co-productive planning theorists have yet to incorporate a more historical view of the approach. Peter Hall's 'City of Sweat Equity' cases of resident-planned and built *barridas* in Lima, and Christopher Alexander's pattern language experiments in Berkeley demonstrate a co-productive perspective, where the state may or may not have a role in plan-making, but people can and will work together to improve their environments (Hall, 2002). This approach aligns with a radically pragmatic perspective. 'To give people help, while denying them a significant part in the action, contributes nothing to the development of the individual' (Alinsky, 1972, p 123). Conceptually, co-production through crowdsourcing could foster both self-development and organizational strengthening.

However, co-productive planning theory is nascent, as are substantial evaluations of crowdsourcing in planning. 'Co-production certainly merits development, but the only way to do this ... is to build theory from case studies, i.e., from contexts' (V. Watson, personal communication, January 27, 2017). Though not without challenges, crowdsourcing might be able to serve both less-developed communities, as well as technologically-savvy areas. Though all three bodies of theory for participatory planning—communicative, collaborative, and co-productive—can be connected to crowdsourcing methods, a critical review of the benefits and limitations of this approach of participation is warranted.

Some could argue that crowdsourcing is merely re-instrumentalizing the planning process by getting community members to develop data that may perpetuate existing power imbalances. However, I argue that a radical perspective on co-production should orient toward meeting, rather than overthrowing, the rules of planning organizations, and should be both productive and fun for participants. These are Alinsky's fourth and sixth rules of tactical engagement. 'Make the enemy live up to their own book of rules' (Alinsky, 1972, p 128) suggests that publics can produce the information meeting planning requirements, that might in some cases counter the findings of the organization. By playing by the planning organizations' rules, advocates can counter the power balance without having to overthrow legal structures. 'A good tactic is one that your people enjoy' (Alinsky, 1972, p 128) involves developing approaches that people do not need to spend very long to learn and take some delight in the process. Wells's conception of actualizing civic styles shows that smartphone-based participation, in the mid-and-late 2010s, supports individual expression and experience in support of organizational goals, and are capable of effecting change.

Co-production is not a new concept for planning, but the use of information systems and online tools supports working together in new ways—potentially increasing the number and geographic scale of participants. Afzalan and Muller's (2018) review and guidance for implementing online participatory technologies begins with defining objectives. This chapter suggests that planners can broadly characterize these objectives as aligning with communicative, collaborative, and co-productive approaches. Either participants or planners could lead a co-productive approach to online participation, but defining objectives can help guide choices about how to implement and evaluate digital co-production. The preceding decade of online planning participation synthesized by Afzalan and Muller shows a wide range of approaches to conduct and evaluate online participation in general, but few studies involve co-production where participants '*do* some of the work of planning, instead of just *talking* about it' (Griffin and Jiao, 2019a).

Aligned with recent emphasis in evaluating on-ground outcomes of planning (Fainstein, 2010) versus communicative process outputs, co-productive planning invites analysis of planning impacts. However, plans often take a decade or more to implement, since intervening changes including political leadership and even neighborhood structure can hamper alignment of planning actions to specific outcomes. However, bike sharing systems provide a relatively simple and expedient example of digital co-production.

Planning processes for bike share systems in the United States during 2012–16 were mostly planner-led approaches that incorporated online map platforms for the public to suggest where to place bike share stations, described in geography and planning literature as public participation geographic information systems (PPGIS). Planners incorporated this online map input with traditional public meetings and workshops to achieve broad and detailed involvement. Analysis of planning bike share in New York (Citi Bike), and Chicago (Divvy) showed limits to the use of PPGIS for digital co-production (Griffin and Jiao, 2019a). Use of two metrics that relate the proximity of bike share station suggestions to actual placement by the systems show implementation of between 5 and 17 percent of suggestions (Griffin and Jiao, 2019a). However, the study suggested that the PPGIS could support learning about the planning process by performing actions, while planners could learn from local knowledge of the streetscape to locate bike share stations. This work supports the emergence of co-productive participation in planning as an impactful approach, but one that remains limited by communicative, collaborative, and power-based constraints—still more pragmatic than radical.

Co-production is important because it offers an approach to reconsider local communities as not only the site but also the means of producing information for planning. However, there are several challenges to such an approach. New tools and techniques in planning—including those developed ostensibly for democratic, rather than authoritarian ends (Mumford, 1964)—do not guarantee even empowerment or even access to participation. Further, high-technology approaches may exacerbate perceptions of valuable participation, even as the information gathered could have severe problems for use in planning, leading to 'idiotic data' rather than improving the smartness of cities (Tironi and Valderrama, 2018). The breakdowns in accurate and useful information shown in Tironi and Valderrama's case study assume a strong separation between the creators of the technology and its users, which is the case in most urban planning instances. However, Haklay has framed these problems, termed 'Neogeography and the delusion of democratization' as both a challenge and a way forward, noting the 'separation between a technological elite and a wider group of uninformed, laboring participants who are not empowered through the use of the technology' (Haklay, 2013). Haklay proposed an approach toward hacking, understood as 'the ability to alter and change the meaning and use of a specific technological system.'

Co-production provides approaches to both perform action-oriented planning as introduced in this chapter and to understand how information is translated into power through the legitimization of planning as a socio-technical process—that is, an inseparable web of human and computational actions and information. Sheila Jasanoff uses the term *technocracy* as revolving 'around the premise that expert "technocrats" might seize the reins of power without respect for public preferences' (Jasanoff, 2017, p 261). This chapter framed co-production as an emerging tradition in participatory planning, and shows how new technologies do not determine co-productive planning, but instead are co-constructed through social processes of participatory planning that also incorporate digital tools involving social interactions that may not be visible without constructivist interrogation. Co-productive planning incorporates knowledge from the participatory traditions of communicative and collaborative planning while supporting development and critique of expert and lay-produced information for planning.

Across these different approaches, whether considering a top-down perspective or a co-production model, studies of planning involved disparate phenomena extending over time and space in a way that the natural sciences do not have to manage in a similar fashion. If the goal of learning from individual cases is to be able to develop inferences about different situations, the quality of those inferences is dependent not only on the study design, but also how we delve into the quality of the validity of the findings. Establishing transport truths requires engaging and testing theories with more than a single approach.

Meta-inferences for transport truths

While deductive and inductive methods are appropriate for developing meta inferences, abductive theoretical reasoning is the approach emphasized in critical realist studies. By moving between empirical analysis of events in redescribing initial findings based on previous theories, applied critical realist ontologies allow identification of the causal mechanisms and changes in social structures (Melia, 2020). This type of analysis is rarely supported by either quantitative or qualitative, but rather, taking both together to be able to refine explanations of what's happening in transport to identify not only what causal mechanisms are, but how to transform them towards human thriving. Yet validity is key to evaluate the legitimacy of any mixed methods approach.

Critical realists apply mixed methods to allow comparison between findings from the combination of methods, rather than a single approach. Following a critical realist ontology that reality exists, but it's not fully knowable, meta-inferences tie empirical observation with iterative theory building about how different transport, social, and environmental mechanisms interact to produce particular results. Researchers trying to create causal explanations of specific social phenomena may nonetheless adopt an 'attitude of epistemological modesty' to restrain the power of any individual study to define a truth (Runde and de Rond, 2010, p 433). Studies that attend to issues of validity and reliability in using a critical realist approach may nonetheless find how the 'logic of retroduction can guide a productive and dynamic interplay between methods involving constant comparison in [a critical realism] inspired, mixed-methods approach' (Zachariadis et al, 2013, p 877).

In the domain of transport planning, the adoption of mixed methods, incorporating both qualitative and quantitative paradigms, is often heralded as a means to triangulate 'reality.' While this methodological pluralism does hold the promise of a more nuanced understanding of complex systems, it is fraught with limitations that may hinder pragmatic and timely decision-making.

One of the foremost limitations pertains to epistemological discord. Mixed methods often require the integration of data, interpretations, and even ontological perspectives that may not necessarily align. For example, qualitative data on community sentiment towards a new transport project may be in tension with quantitative indicators like cost-effectiveness or transport efficiency. This discord can lead to an analytical impasse, making it difficult for planners to coherently synthesize findings and devise actionable plans.

Second, the triangulation of 'reality' through mixed methods assumes that the concept of 'reality' is singular and can be fully apprehended. However, the ontological perspective of critical realism suggests that reality is layered, with deep structural mechanisms that may not be directly observable. Given this, the reliance on data triangulation to capture 'reality' might perpetuate an illusion of comprehensiveness, while essential, non-empirical elements remain elusive.

A third limitation is the time and resources required for robust mixed-methods research. Transport planning often operates under time-sensitive conditions, needing swift solutions to alleviate congestion, improve safety, or meet other pressing needs. The protracted timescales often associated with conducting rigorous mixed-methods studies can be a bottleneck in the planning process, especially when rapid interventions are required.

Now, let's turn to the crux of the matter—the necessity for pragmatic solutions. Transport planning exists in a space of applied policy, often dictated by the urgency to deliver projects that have immediate social, economic, and environmental implications. In this context, the pursuit of an elusive, comprehensive 'truth' through mixed methods can be a hindrance rather than a help. It becomes imperative to acknowledge that while we strive for the most accurate representation of reality, this 'truth' is perhaps not entirely knowable, at least not within actionable timeframes.

Thus, a balance must be struck. Planners need to recognize the inherent limitations in their methodological approaches and make decisions that, while perhaps not capturing the full complexity of the underlying reality, do address the most pressing and empirically substantiated aspects of the problem at hand. In doing so, they walk a fine line—between the rigor of mixed-methods research and the practical exigencies that demand swift and effective solutions. Therefore, the art and science of transport planning lie not just in triangulating a multi-faceted reality but in navigating the ontological, epistemological, and pragmatic constraints that bound the field.

Contributions

If the two case study chapters attempted to show how critical realism can be applied to attempt to uncover the causal mechanisms of transport truths, this chapter has explained more about how a researcher can distill these ideas to improve the results of in-depth analysis and pointed directions towards further research that can help guide a research design that continually improves upon its predecessors.

Sequencing data collection is important because doing so thoughtfully allows a researcher to evaluate whether reasoning or convenience guide decisions of priority in a study. When few theories or studies exist about a topic, descriptive empirical investigation can guide more in-depth inquiry about why or how a transport phenomenon occurs may be most appropriate. Yet, when researchers start from a platform of existing knowledge, then new theories or explanations may be needed through qualitative inquiry as a priority. There are some contexts in which both may be pursued at the same time, and meta-inferences can arise from a fully integrated, mixed-methods study (Creamer, 2018). This cognitive pushback between whether one is exploring or explaining phenomena can help guide the type of designs that lead to advancements upon previous knowledge.

Co-production, thanks to technologies such as crowdsourcing, suggest new ways for researchers and practitioners to work with communities towards self-improvement. In the example of crowdsourced bicycle volumes and route quality, this summarization of my previous work suggests that co-productive approaches can be both efficient in terms of time and resources, while leading to better explanations of transport behaviors and how to address them through planning than previously available. Digital co-production may also risk forms of technological hegemony, if transport researchers and planners fail to actively engage this area of innovation to lead toward beneficial, or even emancipatory results. However, there are relatively few cases of digital co-production to yet identify all of the characteristics that would lead to positive results.

Finally, this chapter shows how meta-inferences can enable the extension of empirical and theoretical knowledge to logical abduction for transport truths. Researchers can apply mixed methods to identify quantitative evaluations of events, and then evaluate how those findings support or conflict with qualitative descriptions of how the mechanism can cause change in reality. Through redescription and retroduction, critical realists can synthesize explanations that are most likely at play.

Box 7.1: Triangulation takeaways for practice

- Full knowledge of all factors impacting transport phenomena is impossible, but integrating qualitative and quantitative data may uncover important truths.
- Sequence of thinking about transport problems and data matters. Use knowledge of the transport issues to guide how to design a solution.
- Cut through dissonance of combinations of qualitative and quantitative data by reflecting on how results could impact communities.

8

Conclusion: Speaking
Truths to Power

Powerful research is about how we turn knowledge into action, both during and after a study. This chapter reviews the findings across the case studies, suggesting a growing emphasis on a critical realism approach to knowledge production may emphasize qualitative and mixed methods in transport to address systems of power for social and environmental progress. However, it provides counterpoints that knowledge of wicked problems may never be fully uncovered, and that mixed methods may over-complicate and needlessly delay finding suitable answers in some contexts. This chapter provides practical tools to assess how transport research is used in policy making, centered on how it is communicated. The concluding section points to the progress and problems that remain for researchers and scholars seeking transport truths.

A slow, steady rise for critical realism?

Traditional transport research has predominantly gravitated towards either positivist frameworks, which emphasize empirical observation and quantifiable variables, or interpretive frameworks, which prioritize subjective experience and contextual understanding. In this duality, critical realist approaches have been comparatively underutilized. Critical realism, a philosophy that combines elements of positivism and interpretivism, posits that while an objective reality exists, our understanding of it is always mediated by social, cultural, and linguistic factors. In other words, it seeks to understand not just the 'what' but also the 'why'—the underlying mechanisms and structures that give rise to observable phenomena.

The absence of critical realist approaches in traditional transport research can be seen as a limitation, especially when tackling wicked problems—complex issues that are difficult to define and solve due to their interdependencies, uncertainties, and multifaceted nature. Transport issues like urban congestion, environmental sustainability, and social equity in access to transportation are classic examples of wicked problems. They involve multiple stakeholders, varying scales of impact, and a host of economic, social, and technological factors.

The critical realist approach can provide a nuanced lens for investigating these wicked problems in several ways. Critical realism allows researchers to explore the multiple layers of reality, from the empirical to the actual and the real. This ontological depth is particularly useful in understanding the underlying structures and mechanisms that contribute to complex issues. Second, traditional approaches may stop at identifying correlations between variables, but critical realism pushes researchers to probe deeper into causal mechanisms, thereby getting closer to potential solutions for multifaceted problems. Integrating multiple methods aligns well with a critical realist ontology (Creamer, 2018). Quantitative methods can capture the empirical patterns and trends, while qualitative methods can delve into the experiences, perceptions, and contextual factors. This integrative approach is often necessary for grappling with the complexity of wicked problems. Third, wicked problems are not static; they evolve over time due to the interplay of various factors. Critical realism's emphasis on change and process over time complements the need for dynamic solutions. Finally, by uncovering the deeper structures and causal relationships at play, critical realist research can offer more substantive insights for policy formulation and implementation, rather than mere technical fixes. In summary, incorporating critical realist approaches into transport research can contribute to a more comprehensive, nuanced, and potentially transformative understanding of wicked problems. The framework encourages methodological pluralism and offers the conceptual depth needed to explore complex issues, making it particularly pertinent for contemporary challenges in the transport domain.

Critiques of critical realism offer valuable cautionary perspectives that could influence its application in transport research and planning. One primary critique is that the ontological commitment to identifying underlying structures and mechanisms might lead researchers down a path of speculative theorizing that could diverge from empirical evidence. In transport planning, where policy interventions are often time-sensitive and constrained by budgetary considerations, an overemphasis on exploring underlying realities could result in less immediate, actionable insights. Moreover, the quest to uncover these deeper structures could inadvertently marginalize other, more pragmatic research approaches that focus on empirical observations and immediate solutions.

Another critique lies in the methodological implications of critical realism's assumption that reality is not fully knowable. If researchers approach transport problems from this epistemological standpoint, there might be a tendency to be overly cautious or indecisive, perhaps advocating for ongoing inquiry rather than decisive action. This could slow down the policy implementation process and potentially hinder immediate improvements in transport systems. Additionally, this viewpoint may lead to a form of relativism where multiple perspectives are given equal weight in the name of acknowledging different facets of 'reality.' In practice, this could complicate the decision-making process and dilute the focus from empirically effective solutions.

The notion that reality is not fully knowable also raises ethical concerns, particularly in participatory planning frameworks. If the structures and mechanisms being investigated are open to interpretation, there's a risk that powerful stakeholders might manipulate these interpretations to suit their agendas, thereby undermining the equitable distribution of transport services and amenities. This epistemological ambiguity could create a power vacuum that might be filled by those with the resources to shape public perception of what the 'underlying structures' of transport problems actually are.

However, acknowledging that reality is not fully knowable also has its merits. It keeps researchers and planners open to alternative explanations and solutions, inviting a pluralistic, multidisciplinary approach that could yield innovative solutions to complex, 'wicked' problems. It also fosters humility in scientific inquiry, promoting continuous engagement with the community and stakeholders, and iterative adjustments in policy interventions.

Therefore, while the critiques of critical realism serve as important caveats, they don't necessarily undermine its utility in transport research and planning. Instead, they highlight the need for a balanced approach that combines the depth of critical realism with the pragmatism of other research paradigms to create an effective, equitable, and responsive transport system.

Uses and misuses of transport research in policy

Transport research often plays a pivotal role in shaping public policy, providing data-driven insights, predictive models, and evaluations of existing initiatives. Policy makers rely on this research to make informed decisions about infrastructure investments, traffic regulations, public transportation planning, and sustainability efforts. When used appropriately, transport research can be transformative, helping cities and countries build efficient, equitable, and environmentally sustainable transportation systems. For example, evidence-based policy measures such as congestion pricing in cities like London and Singapore were informed by meticulous transport research and have shown notable success in reducing traffic and improving air quality.

However, the misuse or selective interpretation of transport research can lead to flawed policy decisions with long-lasting repercussions. One common pitfall is the over-reliance on quantitative data at the expense of qualitative insights. Chapter 5 showed exactly this situation in the case of forecasting traffic volumes at I35 in Austin TX. Policy makers and technologically skilled traffic forecasters coordinated to devise the forecast that practically guaranteed a high traffic future that was then used to create a purpose and need statement to guide an environmental review. While quantitative models can offer robust forecasts and identify statistical correlations, they might miss out on the nuanced human factors that qualitative research can illuminate, such as commuter behavior or community preferences. This one-sided approach can result in policies that look good on paper but fail to account for actual human experiences and thus do not achieve their intended outcomes.

Another issue is the politicization of transport research. Policy makers may cherry-pick findings that align with their political agendas while ignoring other crucial data, leading to policies that may be suboptimal or even counterproductive. For instance, a policy decision to expand road infrastructure might be justified through research showing increased car usage, while disregarding other research advocating for more sustainable modes of transport, like cycling or public transit, based on environmental concerns. Chapter 6 showed potential risks for choosing projects, and partners and infrastructure, that could lead to short term solutions but have possible long term impacts related to more complex, wicked phenomena like the autonomy of decisions in independence from foreign debt cycles.

Furthermore, the gap between academic research timelines and the speed of policy-making processes can result in research being either hastily applied or becoming outdated. Research that is rushed may lack rigor, while findings that emerge too late may become irrelevant, as the policy window has already closed. Lastly, the misuse can also be a consequence of poor communication between researchers and policy makers, where the latter might not fully comprehend the limitations and assumptions underlying a study, leading to misinterpretation and misapplication of the research findings.

In essence, while transport research has the potential to significantly influence and improve policy outcomes, its impact is contingent on how well it is integrated into the decision-making process. Misuse or misinterpretation not only undermines the credibility of the research but also risks the implementation of ineffective or even detrimental policies.

Assessing the limitations of quantitative and qualitative methods

Quantitative transport research, grounded in empirical methods and statistical analysis, is lauded for its ability to provide generalizable findings. It excels in offering a macro view of transport phenomena by analyzing large datasets, thereby enabling the identification of patterns, correlations, and trends. However, its limitations are palpable when nuance and context are needed. Quantitative research often assumes a level of homogeneity among populations and contexts that might not exist, thereby potentially oversimplifying complex issues. The focus on measurable variables can exclude important but intangible aspects like human behavior, cultural factors, and psychological elements, which can be critical for understanding the multifaceted nature of transport systems. Further, the positivist underpinning can create a rigidity that fails to accommodate the complexities and fluidity of real-world transport issues.

Qualitative transport research, on the other hand, excels where quantitative methods falter—namely, in understanding the context, the 'why' behind the patterns, and the lived experiences of individuals. It allows for greater exploration of complexity, behavior, and mechanisms, often bringing forth perspectives that could be overlooked in a purely quantitative approach. However, qualitative research has its own set of limitations. First, its findings are generally not generalizable due to smaller sample sizes and subjective methodologies. Its interpretive nature can lead to biases, both on the part of the researcher and the respondents, thereby potentially affecting the validity of the results. Moreover, qualitative research is often resource-intensive, requiring specialized skills for data collection and analysis, like interviews, focus groups, or ethnographic studies, which can be both time-consuming and costly. The richness of qualitative data, while a strength, can also be a limitation when it comes to synthesizing findings and drawing clear, actionable conclusions.

In summary, while both quantitative and qualitative methods have much to offer in the domain of transport research, each comes with its own set of limitations that researchers must navigate. The ideal approach often lies in a judicious mix of the two, aimed at leveraging the strengths of each while mitigating their respective limitations.

Toward a co-productive approach for transport truths

This study advances a new framework for evaluating participation in planning for a digital age, including accessibility, transparency, representativeness, social learning, and legitimacy. Taken together, the approach can consider both the immediate impacts of the work of planners and publics, in addition to a reference for considering the implementation of a plan through medium and long-term impact. An approach can be considered legitimate if planners show the public how their input will be used, and follow through their words. Accessibility is concerned not only with the geography of participation, but whether people can digitally or physically engage with the process. Social learning represents encouragement of participants to gain knowledge likely to be useful beyond the present issue at hand, under the notion that people's time should be respected as individuals, and as conduits for others in their homes and communities to build continuous and impactful engagement. A transparent process offers insight on both immediate use of information for decision-making, in addition to feedback and reporting how participants impact the implementation of projects over time. Digital access is a cornerstone for transparency in a contemporary civic context. Representativeness refers to the relative match between people involved in the process and the communities that stand to be impacted by a planning process in the present and future.

This framework suggests the importance of transparency and accessibility need in transportation research and planning. Both cases in Austin, Texas and Banjul, Gambia suggest instances where empirical analysis was available but organizational leaders are in a challenging situation to be able to choose which information is appropriate to share with the community at a given time, recognizing that one decision might lead to differences in support of the final project.

I suggest a change to a co-productive approach in how transport projects are planned and coordinated with communities. Rather than just open meetings laws that require discourse, I favor a more radical transparency that forms the basis of accessibility, representation of the communities, social learning, and ultimately, legitimacy. Modern digital infrastructures can support the radical transparency at the root of open government concepts. However, previous governments and research organizations have never fully implemented, nor tested the results of how radical openness and constant feedback facilitated by online engagement might transform transport planning results. Much of the critique I found from audiences in Austin related either to a lack of forthright information coming from the transport agency or from public ignorance of what processes are actually on the table for determining the region's future. I use that strong term ignorance not because the public has not worked hard to delve within the government processes but because the lack of feedback makes it nearly impossible for an average community member to process and engage meaningfully when a meeting is held. No wonder people think public participation as practiced in the United States is a waste of time. Perhaps more nimble and flexible opportunities in locations that are highly digitally connected such as The Gambia might serve as a useful pilot for a more robust public engagement system that treats people as intelligent arbiters of community transport infrastructure futures.

Table 8.1 frames these key questions along a gradation of observability. Access may be the clearest to ascertain because it is fundamentally about whether information is discoverable. In order to evaluate transparency of the information, an observer must gain knowledge not only of what is easily seen, but also what information may be hidden within an agency's files or conversations. Representativeness should be assessed not only by the people reflected in public meetings, but also in their relative impacts to the resulting plans or improvements. Social learning can be more difficult to assess, though simple before-and-after questionnaires may be useful.

Table 8.1: Co-productive critical assessment of public planning

	Criteria	Starting question
Events	1. Accessibility	Can publics find information from agencies about the plan and how to get involved?
	2. Transparency	What proportion of the key agency information is readily available to publics?
	3. Representativeness	Does knowledge from all people impacted by a project guide the agency's process and products?
	4. Social learning	How are publics and agency learning from each other?
Structures	5. Legitimacy	Do the agency's planning processes, laws, and implementation align to meet public needs?

Legitimacy intentionally lacks contrast in the figure, as it may in real life. Though it seems intuitive, discerning whether a planning process or outcome are legitimate can require revealing agency and public intentions, rather than just observable actions. Despite the effort to frame starting questions simply, assessing each of these criteria may end up being an independent study. By framing the approach clearly, this may also help agencies and publics co-produce transport planning processes that support these criteria by design.

As a hypothetical, but a plausible example, consider a medium-sized metropolitan planning organization (MPO) responsible for developing a comprehensive, cooperative, and continuing planning process for a region. The MPO might invite the public to contribute by using a smartphone platform that integrates data on participants' bicycling trips with their comments on desired improvements, for example. To provide ongoing evaluation of the process before fully integrating results, the MPO could survey participants using this framework as a guide for developing questions. Accessibility questions could target ease-of-use regarding the app, including concerns of potentially using participants' smartphone data plans. Transparency could be evaluated by asking whether participants could view new information used in plan development through the process. Representation questions could include demographic and geographic information, in addition to open-ended questions about how to pull in other communities to participate. Social learning questions might include both factual questions to test knowledge, in addition to subjective elements that allow self-reporting of new knowledge gained through using the platform. Legitimacy might be assessed through questions related to a perceived likelihood of implementing public suggestions, or a Likert-scale (disagree–agree) response to perceived legitimacy, perhaps including participants' previous participatory transportation planning experiences. The survey could be as brief as five or ten questions and include only a sample of all participants, or researchers could be involved to improve the analysis and robustness. A brief report targeted toward agency decision-makers could help frame the real and perceived quality of the co-produced information to inform planning decisions, in addition to serving as a reference for continuous improvement of participatory planning. This hypothetical is only one plausible approach to applying the framework for evaluating co-productive planning, and future researchers could develop more robust approaches to evaluate new developments in crowdsourcing, machine learning, or human-centered participation outputs and outcomes.

Creating this feedback approach can start with a small pilot project. Given a context in which people are open to exploring new methods, if it can do so without feeling like their livelihoods are on the line based on the results of the planning solutions, then perhaps people could come together to try. Huge projects such as freeways and airports are not the right context to scale new approaches that are untested. Nowhere are they necessarily the context for exploring what the anticipatory transportation system might look like. Perhaps smaller, nuanced solutions for walking and biking in exploring infrastructure solutions for emerging micro mobility modes might be more appropriate.

New media for transport truths

Media innovation holds significant promise for revitalizing both public engagement and analytical methods in the domain of transport research. Advances in technologies such as augmented and virtual reality, big data analytics, and social media platforms offer new paradigms for community involvement and data collection.

Augmented reality (AR) and virtual reality (VR) can offer immersive experiences that facilitate better public understanding of proposed transport projects or changes. For instance, before the implementation of a new public transit route or bike lane, AR and VR could provide citizens with a virtual experience of how these changes would impact their daily commute. This enhanced form of public engagement could elicit more informed feedback, which would be invaluable for planners and decision-makers.

Big data and machine learning algorithms provide robust tools for transport analysis by aggregating and interpreting massive datasets from diverse sources. Traditional methods of transport analysis often rely on surveys and traffic counts, which are limited in scope and can become outdated quickly. In contrast, real-time data from social media, GPS services, and Internet of Things (IoT) devices can provide a dynamic, comprehensive picture of transport behaviors and trends. Machine learning algorithms can analyze this data to identify patterns or anomalies that might not be discernible through traditional methods, such as the early detection of bottlenecks in a transport system or subtle shifts in commuter behavior in response to external factors like economic change or environmental conditions.

Social media platforms offer another layer of public engagement that transcends the limitations of traditional town halls or public meetings. Platforms such as Twitter or specialized community forums can serve as real-time feedback mechanisms where citizens can express their views, report issues, or even contribute to data collection. Citizen-sourced data, sometimes termed 'crowdsourcing,' can be integrated into transport analysis, allowing for a form of co-production of knowledge where both experts and the public contribute to a richer understanding of issues.

Innovative narrative and visualization techniques, powered by advanced graphic design and data visualization software, can also serve to make transport data more understandable and engaging to the public. Interactive dashboards and infographics can break down complex data into digestible, actionable insights, fostering a more informed public discourse.

Overall, media innovation offers a multifaceted approach to elevating both public engagement and transport analysis. By integrating these advanced technologies and platforms into traditional methodologies, researchers and policy makers can enhance the quality of their work while also fostering a more participatory, democratic process.

Assessing power and progress

The physical definition of power relates energy and work production to time. If a physical notion of power is transferable to urban planning, this would suggest that more energy (through more participants) has the potential to create more powerful planning. However, this assumes that all actors pull in the same direction, which practice suggests is seldom the case. Might crowdsourcing—an online co-production method to facilitate bottom-up contributions to top-down ideas (Brabham, 2013)—offer a venue for the exploration of processes and outcomes that might support empowerment? Research on digitally-mediated practices to support co-production of information for urban planning differ from definitions centered on mass creativity to solve a problem (Brabham, 2013; Afzalan and Muller, 2018). Manuel Castells's development of network power theory still needs to be broken down into more empirical and practical approaches to be able to transform transport planning. Critical realist research, if integrated in the larger scope of transport planning, could illuminate more of the opportunities to harness democratic and emancipatory approaches that align transport needs with our large-scale applications of capital resources and infrastructure.

In assessing power dynamics in infrastructure projects in The Gambia through a decolonial lens, one must integrate historical, economic, and socio-political dimensions. Building upon the theoretical frameworks established by Achille Mbembe and other scholars in decolonial studies, it's vital to critically examine who stands to benefit from such projects, how they are executed, and what their long-term ramifications are for the local populace and culture. Understanding The Gambia's colonial and postcolonial history provides a foundational layer for this assessment. The historical context elucidates existing power structures that can, either overtly or covertly, be perpetuated through infrastructure projects. This analysis serves to reveal whether these projects function as a continuation of colonial legacies, where foreign powers often exert influence to the detriment of local agency.

Equally important is an inquiry into the economic facets of the infrastructure projects. Decolonial theory demands a focus on whether such projects reinforce dependency on high-income countries or global financial institutions. The nature of the funding—whether it is a loan, grant, or investment—can influence the sovereignty of The Gambia, potentially binding the country to external political or economic agendas. The decolonial perspective argues that economic structures are not neutral but inherently coded with power relations that often reproduce colonial forms of domination and exploitation.

On a socio-political level, a decolonial lens compels us to scrutinize how these infrastructure projects intersect with local culture, governance, and citizen participation. Is the local populace involved in decision-making processes, or are these decisions unilaterally imposed by either foreign entities or local elites? Furthermore, how do these projects impact local cultural and social ecosystems? Decolonial theories, including Mbembe's concept of the 'postcolony,' emphasize that sustaining local cultures and social practices is not just about the preservation of tradition but is also a form of resistance and agency in the face of global capitalist and neocolonial forces.

Finally, examining the environmental impact of these projects also has decolonial implications. Environmental degradation disproportionately impacts marginalized communities and perpetuates existing inequalities, often echoing the extractive policies of colonial regimes. Therefore, assessing the environmental sustainability of infrastructure projects is integral to a comprehensive decolonial analysis. From a decolonial standpoint, analyzing power dynamics in The Gambia's infrastructure projects requires a complex, inter-disciplinary approach that extends beyond merely evaluating economic benefits or technical feasibility. It demands a nuanced understanding of how such projects can either perpetuate or disrupt existing power relations that have been shaped by historical, economic, and socio-political factors.

To assess progress in addressing power dynamics in infrastructure projects in The Gambia from a decolonial standpoint, one must employ a multidimensional framework that accounts for both quantitative and qualitative metrics. On the quantitative side, traditional indicators such as the rate of return on investment, job creation, and infrastructural efficiency are essential but inadequate by themselves. From a decolonial perspective, it is crucial to measure the degree of local ownership, both literal and figurative. How many local entities are engaged as primary stakeholders in the projects? Are local materials and resources being used, thereby strengthening internal economies rather than promoting external dependency? These questions illuminate the extent to which projects are genuinely designed to benefit The Gambia in the long term rather than serving as conduits for external capital and influence.

However, quantitative metrics can sometimes obscure nuanced social and cultural implications. Therefore, qualitative assessments are equally vital. This involves understanding local perceptions of these projects through community consultations and ethnographic studies. One might assess how well local knowledge and cultural practices are integrated into the planning and execution of these projects. In line with Mbembe's theories, the ability of the infrastructure projects to sustain and nourish local cultures is a crucial indicator of decolonial progress. For example, do the projects honor or disrupt local spatial arrangements, communal relationships, and traditional ways of knowing and being? These qualitative factors offer insights into whether the projects are empowering the local population or perpetuating hierarchical, colonial-era dynamics. It's also essential to monitor how these projects intersect with existing forms of governance and whether they amplify or mitigate socio-political disparities within the country.

Additionally, longitudinal studies and post-project audits offer a mechanism for sustained assessment. Progress is not only a function of immediate outcomes but also of long-term sustainability and adaptability. Decolonial progress involves scrutinizing whether these infrastructure projects leave behind a legacy of capability and agency, rather than debt and dependency. Are skills and technologies transferred to local entities, thereby enabling future self-sustained projects? Is there a reduction in reliance on external loans or aid, signifying a move towards economic sovereignty? Moreover, has the environmental impact been assessed and managed in a manner that accords with local values and sustainable practices? Evaluating these aspects over a protracted period allows for a more comprehensive understanding of whether the projects have engendered a form of development that is aligned with decolonial principles. In summary, assessing progress through a decolonial lens necessitates a balanced, multifaceted approach that captures economic, socio-political, cultural, and temporal dimensions.

Contributions

In this book, I have contended that a myopic focus on purely empirical or rational methods in transport planning is insufficient. Instead, the chapter advocates for a multi-pronged approach, encapsulated by four key paradigms: sociotechnical seeing, mixed methods, critical realism, and a strong ethical underpinning. By shifting focus from mere technical aspects to a broader understanding, which includes social and cultural dimensions, the chapter nudges political leaders and planners towards a more holistic understanding of transport systems. It calls upon them to question existing norms and recognize the inevitability of bias, thereby encouraging a more nuanced and responsive approach to transport planning.

Challenges and opportunities come with leveraging big data and machine learning for transport planning. While big data offers tantalizing possibilities for understanding user behavior and predicting future trends, it inherently risks exclusion and representation biases. This presents a dilemma for political leaders: how to reconcile the allure of data-driven policies with the potential of such policies to perpetuate systemic inequities. Chapter 3 also calls for a rigorous blend of randomized controlled trials and natural experiments, particularly underlining the need for interdisciplinary approaches to tackle complex challenges.

To set up case studies in this book, the role of qualitative and mixed-methods research methods in transport planning comes to the fore. By weaving in case studies, such as interviews with Gambian students and a pedestrian bridge project in Austin, the chapter demonstrates how qualitative research can unearth nuanced insights that quantitative methods often miss. Given the rise of smart cities and data-centric governance models, the chapter calls for an ethical recalibration, urging political leaders and planners to ensure that their decisions are grounded in a nuanced, humanistic understanding of transport systems. It also hints at the promise and limitations of using artificial intelligence in qualitative research, suggesting that while AI can handle tasks like dictation, it has yet to make meaningful contributions to theory-building exercises. Transport planning needs to move beyond its traditional reliance on purely quantitative or technocratic paradigms. For political leaders and planners, the call to action is clear: adopt a multi-disciplinary, ethically-grounded approach that respects both data and the human stories behind the numbers. This balanced approach not only makes for more informed decisions but also engenders a more participatory, equitable, and effective transport system.

In the context of transportation planning, incorporating critical realism's ontological perspective allows for a more nuanced and transformative understanding of systemic complexities. Critical realism postulates that reality consists of multiple layers that are not always directly observable but exert causal influences. Applied to the practice of transportation planning, this perspective aligns with multi-layered, networked approaches to policy and execution, as well as the theoretical lens of Manuel Castells's network power.

In terms of resolution, the first step involves disentangling the different layers of reality that impact the transport system. For example, in the Austin pedestrian bridge case study, what appeared on the surface to be a straightforward infrastructure project was, in fact, embedded within a complex web of social, political, and economic relations. Critical realism provides a robust framework for delineating these layers, from visible phenomena like budget allocations to deeper, unobservable mechanisms like social trust and political power.

The retroduction stage involves theorizing about the underlying mechanisms that cause observable phenomena. While traditional transport planning often hinges on empirically observable metrics—traffic flow, costs, timetables—critical realism would encourage planners to consider the less visible but equally potent forces at play. It facilitates hypothesizing how the 'network power' dynamics among stakeholders might lead to project delays or successes. In the Austin case, instead of simply noting the delay, planners should engage in retroductive reasoning to understand how different nodes in the network—community sentiments, political incentives, and bureaucratic hurdles—interact and shape the project outcome.

Finally, critical realism's emphasis on the comparison of competing theories allows for a nuanced understanding that incorporates multiple perspectives. For example, while Castells's theory of network power offers a compelling lens for interpreting the Philadelphia-based futures project, it is crucial to compare this with other theoretical frameworks. Could a different model— say, a centralized, top-down planning approach—provide comparable or even superior outcomes? Assessing the relative merits of each perspective adds depth and robustness to our understanding.

In sum, applying critical realism as an ontological perspective enhances our interpretive and analytical capabilities in transportation planning. It urges us to go beyond surface-level observations and engage in a deeper, multi-layered understanding of complex systems. The focus on resolution, retroduction, and theory comparison provides a structured yet flexible framework for incorporating diverse elements, from empirical data to power dynamics, into a cohesive planning strategy. This makes it possible to better navigate the complexities of modern, networked societies in the realm of transportation planning.

> ### Box 8.1: Concluding takeaways for practice
>
> - Transport professionals need to re-think what we think we know to address wicked problems with structural underpinnings.
> - Critical realism is an action-oriented framework, helping separate observable knowledge from invisible, but nonetheless powerful factors impacting society.
> - A co-productive critical assessment approach can be used to both discern transport truths, and to design legitimate planning processes that lead to better futures.

References

Adam, L., Jones, T., and te Brömmelstroet, M. (2018) Planning for cycling in the dispersed city: establishing a hierarchy of effectiveness of municipal cycling policies. *Transportation*, 47(1), DOI: 10.1007/s11116-018-9878-3.

Afzalan, N. and Muller, B. (2018) Online participatory technologies: opportunities and challenges for enriching participatory planning. *Journal of the American Planning Association*, 84(2), pp 162–77.

Akar, G., Fischer, N., and Namgung, M. (2012) Bicycling choice and gender case study: the Ohio State University. *International Journal of Sustainable Transportation*, 7(5), pp 347–65.

Alexiadis, V., Jeannotte, K., and Chandra, A. (2004) *Traffic Analysis Toolbox Volume I: Traffic Analysis Tools Primer* [online], Federal Highway Administration, Available from: https://ops.fhwa.dot.gov/trafficanalysistools/tat_vol1/Vol1_Primer.pdf

Alinsky, S.D. (1972) *Rules for Radicals* (1989 edn), New York: Vintage Books.

Allmendinger, P. and Tewdwr-Jones, M. (2002) The communicative turn in urban planning: unravelling paradigmatic, imperialistic and moralistic dimensions. *Space and Polity*, 6(1), pp 5–24.

Angelidou, M. (2017) The role of smart city characteristics in the plans of fifteen cities. *Journal of Urban Technology*, 24(4), pp 3–28.

Anselin, L. (1995) Local indicators of spatial association-LISA. *Geographical Analysis*, 27(2), pp 93–115.

APA (2021) AICP Code of Ethics and Professional Conduct [online], Available from: https://www.planning.org/ethics/ethicscode/.

Appleyard, B. and Appleyard, D. (2021) *Livable Streets 2.0*, Amsterdam: Elsevier.

Arnstein, S.R. (1969) A ladder of citizen participation. *Journal of the American Institute of Planners*, 35(4), pp 216–24.

ASCE (2021) Code of Ethics [online], Available from: https://www.asce.org/career-growth/ethics/code-of-ethics.

ASPA (2013) Code of Ethics [online], Available from: https://www.aspanet.org/ASPA/ASPA/Code-of-Ethics/Code-of-Ethics.aspx.

Banai, R. (1995) Critical realism, and urban and regional studies. *Environment and Planning B: Planning and Design*, 22(5), pp 563–80.

Banister, D. (2011) Cities, mobility and climate change. *Journal of Transport Geography: Special Section on Alternative Travel Futures*, 19(6), pp 1538–46.

Battista, G.A. and Manaugh, K. (2019) Generating walkability from pedestrians' perspectives using a qualitative GIS method. *Travel Behaviour and Society*, 17, pp 1–7.

Belda, P. (ed) (2006) *The Gambia*, Dublin: Verulam.

Bernier, N. (2022a) I-35 expansion could destroy a 70-unit affordable housing complex: TxDOT didn't notice at first. KUT Radio, Austin's NPR Station [online] March 14, Available from: http://web.archive.org/web/20220404001402/https://www.kut.org/transportation/2022-03-14/i-35-expansion-could-destroy-a-70-unit-affordable-housing-complex-txdot-didnt-notice-at-first.

Bernier, N. (2022b) Double-decker highway coming to South Austin. KUT Radio, Austin's NPR Station [online] November 16, Available from: https://www.kut.org/transportation/2022-11-15/i-35-expansion-south-austin-txdot.

Bhaskar, R. (2010) *Reclaiming Reality*, London: Routledge.

Bhaskar, R. (2013) *A Realist Theory of Science*, London: Routledge.

Bijker, W.E. (1995) *Of Bicycles, Bakelites, and Bulbs: Toward a Theory of Sociotechnical Change*, Boston: MIT Press.

Bittihn, S. and Schadschneider, A. (2021) The effect of modern traffic information on Braess' paradox. *Physica A: Statistical Mechanics and its Applications*, 571(C), DOI: 10.1016/j.physa.2021.125829.

Bogdan, R. and Bilken, S.K. (2003) Qualitative data. In: *Qualitative Research in Education: An Introduction to Theories and Methods*. Boston: Pearson.

Brabham, D.C. (2013) *Crowdsourcing*, Cambridge, MA: MIT Press.

Braess, D., Nagurney, A., and Wakolbinger, T. (2005) On a paradox of traffic planning. *Transportation Science*, 39(4), pp 446–50.

Broach, J., Kothuri, S., Miah, M.M., McNeil, N., Hyun, K., Mattingly, S. et al (2023) Evaluating the potential of crowdsourced data to estimate network-wide bicycle volumes. *Transportation Research Record*, 2678(3), pp 573–89.

Brown, J.R., Morris, E.A., and Taylor, B.D. (2009) Planning for cars in cities: planners, engineers, and freeways in the 20th century. *Journal of the American Planning Association*, 75(2), pp 161–77.

Brunsdon, C., Fotheringham, S., and Charlton, M. (1998) Geographically weighted regression—modelling spatial non-stationarity. *The Statistician*, 47(3), pp 431–43.

Budd, L. and Ison, S. (2020) Responsible transport: a post-COVID agenda for transport policy and practice. *Transportation Research Interdisciplinary Perspectives*, 6, 100151, DOI: 10.1016/j.trip.2020.100151.

Burghardt, K., Uhl, J.H., Lerman, K., and Leyk, S. (2022) Road network evolution in the urban and rural United States since 1900. *Computers, Environment and Urban Systems*, 95, 101803, DOI: 10.48550/arXiv.2108.13407.

Bygstad, B., Munkvold, B.E. and Volkoff, O. (2016). Identifying generative mechanisms through affordances: A framework for critical realist data analysis. *Journal of Information Technology*, 31(1), pp 83–96, https://doi.org/10.1057/jit.2015.13.

Calise, T.V., Dumith, S., DeJong, W., and Kohl, H. (2012) The effect of a neighborhood built environment on physical activity behaviors. *Journal of Physical Activity & Health*, 9(8), pp 1089–98.

Caro, R.A. (1975) *The Power Broker: Robert Moses and the Fall of New York*, New York: Vintage Books.

Castells, M. (2007) Communication, power and counter-power in the network society. *International Journal of Communication*, 1(2007), pp 238–66.

Castells, M. (2011) A network theory of power. *International Journal of Communication*, 5(2011), pp 773–87.

Castells, M. (2013) *Communication Power*, Oxford: Oxford University Press.

Ceesay, E.K., Francis, P.C., Jawneh, S., Njie, M., Belford, C., and Fanneh, M.M. (2021) Climate change, growth in agriculture value-added, food availability and economic growth nexus in the Gambia: a Granger causality and ARDL modeling approach. *SN Business & Economics*, 1(7), pp 1–31.

Checkoway, B. (1994) Paul Davidoff and advocacy planning in retrospect. *Journal of the American Planning Association*, 60(2), pp 139–43.

Chen, P., Zhou, J., and Sun, F. (2017) Built environment determinants of bicycle volume: a longitudinal analysis. *Journal of Transport and Land Use*, 10(1), pp 655–74.

Choi, K., Park, H.J., and Griffin, G.P. (2023) Can shared micromobility replace auto travel? Evidence from the U.S. urbanized areas between 2012 and 2019. *International Journal of Sustainable Transportation*, February, pp 1–9, DOI: 10.1080/15568318.2023.2179444.

CIA (2023) The World Factbook: Gambia [online], Available from: https://www.cia.gov/the-world-factbook/countries/gambia-the/.

City of Austin (2014) Annual Budgets 2014 [online], Available from: https://austintexas.gov/financeonline/finance/financial_docs.cfm?ws=1&pg=1.

City of Austin (2016) RestoreRundberg [online], Available from: https://austintexas.gov/department/restorerundberg.

Cochran, A.L. (2020) Understanding the role of transportation-related social interaction in travel behavior and health: a qualitative study of adults with disabilities. *Journal of Transport & Health*, 19, 100948, DOI: 10.1016/j.jth.2020.100948.

Congress for New Urbanism (2015) Highways to Boulevards CNUText, [online] June 15, Available from: https://www.cnu.org/highways-boulevards/campaign-cities/austin.

Cooper, C. (2007) Successfully changing individual travel behavior: applying community-based social marketing to travel choice. *Transportation Research Record: Journal of the Transportation Research Board*, 2021(1), pp 89–99.

Cope, M. and Elwood, S. (eds) (2009) *Qualitative GIS: A Mixed Methods Approach*, London: Sage.

Creamer, E.G. (2018) *An Introduction to Fully Integrated Mixed Methods Research*, Thousand Oaks, CA: Sage.

CTRMA (2022) Answering Demand, 2021 Annual Report [online], Available from: https://www.mobilityauthority.com/upload/files/publications/2021_Annual_Report_Final.pdf.

Dadashova, B. and Griffin, G.P. (2020) Random parameter models for estimating statewide daily bicycle counts using crowdsourced data. *Transportation Research Part D: Transport and Environment*, 84, 102368, DOI: 10.1016/j.trd.2020.102368.

Das, S. and Griffin, G.P. (2020) Investigating the role of big data in transportation safety. *Transportation Research Record: Journal of the Transportation Research Board*, 2674(6), DOI: 10.1177/0361198120918565.

Das, S., Dutta, A., Lindheimer, T., Jalayer, M., and Elgart, Z. (2019) YouTube as a source of information in understanding autonomous vehicle consumers: natural language processing study. *Transportation Research Record: Journal of the Transportation Research Board*, 2673(8), DOI: 10.1177/0361198119842110.

Davidoff, P. (1965) Advocacy and pluralism in planning. *Journal of the American Institute of Planners*, 31(4), pp 331–8.

Davidson, L. and Sahli, M. (2015) Foreign direct investment in tourism, poverty alleviation, and sustainable development: a review of the Gambian hotel sector. *Journal of Sustainable Tourism*, 23(2), pp 167–87.

De Giorgi, A.U. (2016) *Ancient Antioch: from the Seleucid Era to the Islamic Conquest*, Cambridge: Cambridge University Press.

Deterding, N.M. and Waters, M.C. (2018) Flexible coding of in-depth interviews: a twenty-first-century approach. *Sociological Methods & Research*, 50(2), DOI: 10.1177/0049124118799377.

Dewey, J. (1927) *The Public and its Problem* (1991 print), Athens, Ohio: Swallow Press.

Dill, J., McNeil, N., Broach, J., and Ma, L. (2014) Bicycle boulevards and changes in physical activity and active transportation: findings from a natural experiment. *Preventive Medicine*, 69(S), pp S74–8.

Dill, J., Goddard, T., Monsere, C.M., and McNeil, N. (2015) Can protected bike lanes help close the gender gap in cycling? Lessons from five cities. In: *Compendium of Transportation Research Board 94th Annual Meeting*, Washington, DC: Transportation Research Board of the National Academies.

Dill, J., Ma, J., McNeil, N., Broach, J., and MacArthur, J. (2022) Factors influencing bike share among underserved populations: evidence from three U.S. cities. *Transportation Research Part D: Transport and Environment*, 112, 103471, DOI: 10.1016/j.trd.2022.103471.

Dressel, A., Steinborn, M., and Holt, K. (2014) Get wheelin' in westlawn: mounting a bicycling program in a low-income minority urban community. *Sports*, 2(4), pp 131–9.

Dumbaugh, E. and Rae, R. (2009) Safe urban form: revisiting the relationship between community design and traffic safety. *Journal of the American Planning Association*, 75(3), pp 309–29.

du Toit, J.L. and Mouton, J. (2013) A typology of designs for social research in the built environment. *International Journal of Social Research Methodology*, 16(2), pp 125–39.

DVRPC (2020) Dispatches from alternate futures: exploratory scenarios for Greater Philadelphia [online], Available from: https://www.dvrpc.org/products/20012.

DVRPC (2023) Futures Group [online], Available from: https://www.dvrpc.org/plan/futuresgroup/.

Ehrenfeucht, R. and Loukaitou-Sideris, A. (2010) Planning urban sidewalks: infrastructure, daily life and destinations. *Journal of Urban Design*, 15(4), pp 459–71.

El Esawey, M., Mosa, A.I., and Nasr, K. (2015) Estimation of daily bicycle traffic volumes using sparse data. *Computers, Environment and Urban Systems*, 54, pp 195–203.

Emirates News Agency (2021) OFID's $20m loan to The Gambia will improve connectivity. [online] June 17, Available from: https://www.wam.ae/en/details/1395302944557.

Erlichman, H.J. (2006) Camino del Norte: how a series of watering holes, fords, and dirt trails evolved into Interstate 35. In *Texas' Centennial Series of the Association of Former Students*, College Station, Texas: A&M University Press.

Evans-Cowley, J.S. and Griffin, G.P. (2012) Microparticipation with social media for community engagement in transportation planning. *Transportation Research Record: Journal of the Transportation Research Board*, 2307(1), pp 90–8.

Fainstein, S.S. (2010) The just city. *International Journal of Urban Sciences*, 18(1), 1–18.

Ferenchak, N.N. and Marshall, W.E. (2020) Is bicycling getting safer? Bicycle fatality rates (1985–2017) using four exposure metrics. *Transportation Research Interdisciplinary Perspectives*, 8(3), DOI: 10.1016/j.trip.2020.100219.

Fields, B. and Renne, J.L. (2021) *Adaptation Urbanism and Resilient Communities: Transforming Streets to Address Climate Change*, London: Routledge.

Flahavan, E. (2023) Just noise? Using GPT3 to analyse Google reviews of London police stations. *Behavioural Insights*, [online] January 21, Available from: https://medium.com/behavioural-insights/just-noise-using-gpt3-to-analyse-google-reviews-of-london-police-stations-85603d79d22d.

Flahive, P. (2019) Woman sues Lime and San Antonio for scooter accident. TPR. [online] July 31, Available from: https://www.tpr.org/technol ogy-entrepreneurship/2019-07-31/woman-sues-lime-and-san-antonio-for-scooter-accident.

Flyvbjerg, B. (1998) *Rationality and Power Readings in Planning Theory*, Chicago, IL: The University of Chicago Press.

Flyvbjerg, B. (2006) Five misunderstandings about case-study research. *Qualitative Inquiry*, 12(2), pp 219–45.

Flyvbjerg, B., Skamris Holm, M.K., and Buhl, S.L. (2005) How (in)accurate are demand forecasts in public works projects? The case of transportation. *Journal of the American Planning Association*, 71(2), pp 131–46.

Food and Agriculture Organization of the United Nations (2023) Gambia at a glance [online], Available from: https://www.fao.org/gambia/gam bia-at-a-glance/en/.

Forester, J. (1980) Critical theory and planning practice. *Journal of the American Planning Association*, 46(3), pp 275–86.

Forester, J. (1988) *Planning in the Face of Power*, Berkeley, CA: University of California Press.

Forester, J. (2001) An instructive case-study hampered by theoretical puzzles: critical comments on Flyvbjerg's rationality and power. *International Planning Studies*, 6(3), pp 263–70.

Frank, L.D., Iroz-Elardo, N., MacLeod, K.E., and Hong, A. (2019) Pathways from built environment to health: a conceptual framework linking behavior and exposure-based impacts. *Journal of Transport & Health*, 12 (June 2018), pp 319–35.

Gambia Bureau of Statistics (2021) Transport statistics summary report [online], Available from: https://www.gbosdata.org/downloads-file/407-transport-statistics-summary-report-2021.

Gambia Bureau of Statistics (2023) Tourist arrivals 2023 [online], Available from: https://www.gbosdata.org/data/719-tourist-arrivals/1859-arrivals.

Gao, Y., Qian, S., Li, Z., Wang, P., Wang, F., and He, Q. (2021) Digital twin and its application in transportation infrastructure, In: 2021 IEEE 1st International Conference on Digital Twins and Parallel Intelligence (DTPI), pp 298–301, DOI: 10.1109/DTPI52967.2021.9540108

Geller, R. (2009) Four types of cyclists [online], Available from: https:// www.portlandoregon.gov/transportation/44597?a=237507.

Getis, A. and Ord, J.K. (1992) The analysis of spatial association by use of distance statistics. *Geographical Analysis*, 24(3), pp 189–206.

Goddard, T.B., Handy, S.L., Cao, X., and Mokhtarian, P.L. (2006) Voyage of the SS Minivan: women's travel behavior in traditional and suburban neighborhoods. *Transportation Research Record: Journal of the Transportation Research Board*, 1956(1), pp 141–8.

Golub, A. and Martens, K. (2014) Using principles of justice to assess the modal equity of regional transportation plans. *Journal of Transport Geography*, 41, pp 10–20.

Golub, A., Serritella, M., Satterfield, V., and Singh, J. (2018) *Community-Based Assessment of Smart Transportation Needs in the City of Portland*, Portland, OR: Portland State University.

Goodspeed, R. (2020) *Scenario Planning for Cities and Regions*. Cambridge, MA: Lincoln Institute of Land Policy.

Gössling, S. (2020) Why cities need to take road space from cars – and how this could be done. *Journal of Urban Design*, 25(4), pp 443–8.

Gray, S., O'Brien, O., and Hügel, S. (2016) Collecting and visualizing real-time urban data through city dashboards. *Built Environment*, 42(3), pp 498–509.

Griffin, G.P. (2018) The impact of public involvement in the eventual completion of the North Acres Park pedestrian bridge. Transportation Research Board [online], Available from: https://trid.trb.org/view/1494275

Griffin, G.P. (2019) Sociotechnical Co-production of Planning Information: Opportunities and Limits of Crowdsourcing for the Geography and Planning of Bicycle Transportation, The University of Texas at Austin [online], Available from: https://core.ac.uk/works/34220728/.

Griffin, G.P. (2021) Online workshop on sustainable tourism in The Gambia [online], Available from: https://express.adobe.com/page/cxCSjOmPMZ3xF/.

Griffin, G.P. and Jiao, J. (2015a) Crowdsourcing bicycle volumes: exploring the role of volunteered geographic information and established monitoring methods. *URISA Journal*, 27(1), pp 57–66.

Griffin, G.P. and Jiao, J. (2015b) Where does bicycling for health happen? Analysing volunteered geographic information through place and plexus. *Journal of Transport & Health*, 2(2), pp 238–47.

Griffin, G.P. and Jiao, J. (2019a) Crowdsourcing bike share station locations. *Journal of the American Planning Association*, 85(1), pp 35–48.

Griffin, G.P. and Jiao, J. (2019b) The geography and equity of crowdsourced public participation for active transportation planning. *Transportation Research Record: Journal of the Transportation Research Board*, 2673(1), pp 460–8.

Griffin, G.P., Mulhall, M., Simek, C., and Riggs, W.W. (2020) Mitigating bias in big data for transportation. *Journal of Big Data Analytics in Transportation*, 2(1), pp 49–59.

Gudowsky, N. and Bechtold, U. (2013) The role of information in public participation. *Journal of Public Deliberation*, 9(1), pp 387–94.

Guma, P.K., Akallah, J.A. and Odeo, J.O. (2023). Plug-in urbanism: City building and the parodic guise of new infrastructure in Africa. *Urban Studies*, 00420980231158013, https://doi.org/10.1177/00420980231158013

Guerra, E. (2016) Planning for cars that drive themselves: metropolitan planning organizations, regional transportation plans, and autonomous vehicles. *Journal of Planning Education and Research*, 36(2), pp 210–24.

Guo, N., Jiang, R., Wong, S.C., Hao, Q.Y., Xue, S.Q., Xiao, Y. et al (2020) Modeling the interactions of pedestrians and cyclists in mixed flow conditions in uni- and bidirectional flows on a shared pedestrian-cycle road. *Transportation Research Part B: Methodological*, 139, pp 259–84.

Habermas, J. (1962) *The Structural Transformation of the Public Sphere*, Cambridge, MA: MIT Press.

Habermas, J. (1987) *The Theory of Communicative Action, vol. 2: Lifeworld and System: A Critique of Functionalist Reason* (Thomas McCarthy, translator) Boston: Beacon Press.

Habermas, J. (1990) *Moral Consciousness and Communicative Action*, Cambridge, MA, Polity Press.

Haklay, M. (2013) Neogeography and the delusion of democratisation. *Environment and Planning A*, 45(1), pp 55–69.

Hall, P. (2002) *Cities of Tomorrow* (3rd edn), Oxford: Blackwell.

Handy, S. (2005) Smart growth and the transportation-land use connection: what does the research tell us? *International Regional Science Review*, 28(2), pp 146–67.

Handy, S. and McCann, B. (2011) The regional response to federal funding for bicycle and pedestrian project—an exploratory study. *Journal of the American Planning Association*, 77(1), pp 23–38.

Hansson, E., Mattisson, K., Björk, J., Östergren, P.-O., and Jakobsson, K. (2011) Relationship between commuting and health outcomes in a cross-sectional population survey in southern Sweden. *BMC Public Health*, 11(1), p 834.

Hariton, E. and Locascio, J.J. (2018) Randomised controlled trials—the gold standard for effectiveness research. *BJOG: An International Journal of Obstetrics and Gynaecology*, 125(13), p 1716.

Healey, P. (2003) Collaborative planning in perspective. *Planning Theory*, 2(2), pp 101–23.

Hennink, M. and Kaiser, B.N. (2021) Sample sizes for saturation in qualitative research: A systematic review of empirical tests, *Social Science & Medicine*, 292, 114523, DOI: 10.1016/j.socscimed.2021.114523

Heritage Hills Woodbridge Neighborhood Association (2007) Heritage Hills – WoodBridge neighborhood news, [online], Available from: http://www.main.org/hhwbna/files/Jan2008.pdf.

Heritage Hills Woodbridge Neighborhood Association (2013) Petition: our opposition to the bicycle/pedestrian bridge over Little Walnut Creek at North Acres Park (Segment 16 of Bike Route 57), Change.org [online], Available from: https://www.change.org/p/our-opposition-to-the-bicy cle-pedestrian-bridge-over-little-walnut-creek-at-north-acres-park-segm ent-16-of-bike-route-57.

Herrick, C. (2008) To the west and east of Interstate-35: obesity, philanthropic entrepreneurialism, and the delineation of risk in Austin, Texas. *Environment and Planning A*, 40(11), pp 2715–33.

Hollander, J.B. (2011) Approaching an ideal: using technology to apply collaborative rationality to urban planning processes. *Planning Practice and Research*, 26(5), pp 587–96.

Hommels, A. (2008) *Unbuilding Cities: Obduracy in Urban Sociotechnical Change*, Cambridge, MA: MIT Press.

Horrox, J., Huxley-Reicher, B., and Casale, M. (2022) Highway Boondoggles 7: Wasting Infrastructure Funding on Damaging and Unnecessary Road Projects [online], Available from: https://publicinterestnetwork.org/wp-content/uploads/2022/09/Highway-Boondoggles-7.pdf.

Hosford, K., Laberee, K., Fuller, D., Kestens, Y., and Winters, M. (2020) Are they really interested but concerned? A mixed methods exploration of the Geller bicyclist typology. *Transportation Research Part F: Traffic Psychology and Behaviour*, 75, pp 26–36.

Hosseini, M., Sevtsuk, A., Miranda, F., Cesar, R.M., and Silva, C.T. (2023) Mapping the walk: A scalable computer vision approach for generating sidewalk network datasets from aerial imagery. *Computers, Environment and Urban Systems*, 101, 101950 [online], Available from: https://www.resea rchgate.net/publication/360040812_Mapping_the_Walk_A_Scalable_ Computer_Vision_Approach_for_Generating_Sidewalk_Network_Datas ets_from_Aerial_Imagery.

Innes, J.E. (1998) Information in communicative planning. *Journal of the American Planning Association*, 64(1), p 52.

Innes, J.E. and Booher, D.E. (2018) *Planning With Complexity: An Introduction to Collaborative Rationality for Public Policy* (2nd edn), London: Routledge.

Institute of Transportation Engineers (2010) *Designing Walkable Urban Thoroughfares: A Context Sensitive Approach*, Institute of Transportation Engineers [online], Available from: http://www.ite.org/css/.

International Monetary Fund African Dept. (2021). The Gambia: Staff Report for the 2021 Article IV Consultation, Third Review under the Extended Credit Facility Arrangement, Request for Modification of a Performance Criterion, and Financing Assurances Review—Debt Sustainability Analysis. *IMF Staff Country Reports, 2021*, (265), https://doi.org/10.5089/9781616356767.002.A003.

Jacobs, A.B., Macdonald, E., and Rofé, Y. (2002) *The Boulevard Book: History, Evolution, Design of Multiway Boulevards*, Cambridge, MA: MIT Press.

Jacobs, J. (1961) *The Death and Life of Great American Cities*, New York, Vintage Books.

Jankowski, P., Czepkiewicz, M., Młodkowski, M., Wójcicki, M., and Zwolinski, Z. (2016) Scalability in participatory planning: a comparison of online PPGIS methods with face-to-face meetings. *International Conference on GIScience Short Paper Proceedings*, 1(1), DOI: 10.21433/B3118nh5943s.

Jasanoff, S. (2017) Science and democracy. In: U. Felt, R. Fouché, C. Miller, and L. Smith-Doerr (eds) *The Handbook of Science and Technology Studies* (4th edn) Cambridge, MA: MIT Press, pp 259–88.

Jefferson, G. (2020) Jefferson: how to get San Antonio-Austin passenger rail on track. San Antonio Express-News [online] October 30, Available from: https://www.expressnews.com/business/business_columnists/greg_jefferson/article/Jefferson-The-last-attempt-to-launch-passenger-15688734.php.

Jiang, J.A., Wade, K., Fiesler, C., and Brubaker, J.R. (2021) Supporting serendipity: opportunities and challenges for human-AI collaboration in qualitative analysis. *Proceedings of the ACM on Human-Computer Interaction*, 5(CSCW1), pp 1–23.

Kitchin, R., Lauriault, T.P., and McArdle, G. (2015) Knowing and governing cities through urban indicators, city benchmarking and real-time dashboards. *Regional Studies, Regional Science*, 2(1), pp 6–28.

Knock Software (2017) Ride Report [online], Available from: https://ride.report/.

Kolley, E.A., Xiao, W., and Kai, P. (2017) A study on history of early modern town planning of Banjul. *Landscape Architecture and Regional Planning*, 2(1), pp 23–8.

Krippendorff, K. (2011) Computing Krippendorff's alpha-reliability, Philadelphia, PA: University of Pennsylvania [online], Available from: https://www.asc.upenn.edu/sites/default/files/2021-03/Computing%20Krippendorff%27s%20Alpha-Reliability.pdf.

Krippendorff, K. and Craggs, R. (2016) The reliability of multi-valued coding of data. *Communication Methods and Measures*, 10(4), pp 181–98.

Latour, B. (1990) Technology is society made durable. *The Sociological Review*, 38(1_suppl), pp 103–31.

Laurian, L., Crawford, J., Day, M., Kouwenhoven, P., Mason, G., Ericksen, N. et al (2010) Evaluating the outcomes of plans: theory, practice, and methodology. *Environment and Planning B: Planning and Design*, 37(4), pp 740–57.

Lee, C., Xu, M., Zhu, X., Towne, S.D., Sang, H., Lee, H. et al (2023) Moving to an activity-friendly community can increase physical activity. *Journal of Physical Activity and Health*, 20(11), pp 1058–66.

Lee, K. and Sener, I.N. (2021) Strava Metro data for bicycle monitoring: a literature review. *Transport Reviews*, 41(1), pp 27–47.

Legacy, C. (2010) Investigating the knowledge interface between stakeholder engagement and plan-making. *Environment and Planning A*, 42(11), pp 2705–20.

Lester, T.W. (2022) Replacing truth with social hope and progress with redescription: can the pragmatist philosophy of Richard Rorty help reinvigorate planning? *Journal of Planning Education and Research*, 42(4), 526–38.

Levine, J., Grengs, J., and Merlin, L.A. (2019) *From Mobility to Accessibility: Transforming Urban Transportation and Land-Use Planning*, Ithaca, NY: Cornell University Press.

Levinson, D.M., Marshall, W., and Axhausen, K. (2017) *Elements of Access*, Melbourne: Network Design Lab.

Li, A., Zhao, P., Haitao, H., Mansourian, A., and Axhausen, K.W. (2021) How did micro-mobility change in response to COVID-19 pandemic? A case study based on spatial-temporal-semantic analytics. *Computers, Environment and Urban Systems*, 90, 101703, DOI: 10.1016/j.compenvurbsys.2021.101703.

Liberti, S. (2013) *Land Grabbing: Journeys in the New Colonialism*, London: Verso.

Linovski, O. and Baker, D.M. (2023) Community-designed participation: lessons for equitable engagement in transportation planning. *Transportation Research Record*, 2677(6), pp 172–81.

Lucas, K., Philips, I., and Verlinghieri, E. (2021) A mixed methods approach to the social assessment of transport infrastructure projects. *Transportation*, 49, pp 271–91.

Lugo, A.E. (2013) CicLAvia and human infrastructure in Los Angeles: ethnographic experiments in equitable bike planning. *Journal of Transport Geography*, 30, pp 202–7.

Lusk, A.C., Furth, P.G., Morency, P., Miranda-Moreno, L.F., Willett, W.C., and Dennerlein, J.T. (2011) Risk of injury for bicycling on cycle tracks versus in the street. *Injury Prevention*, 17(2), pp 131–5.

Mackie, P. and Preston, J. (1998) Twenty-one sources of error and bias in transport project appraisal. *Transport Policy*, 5(1), pp 1–7.

Makarewicz, C. and Németh, J. (2017) Are multimodal travelers more satisfied with their lives? A study of accessibility and wellbeing in the Denver, Colorado metropolitan area. *Cities*, 74, pp 179–87.

Mandarano, L. (2015) Civic engagement capacity building: an assessment of the Citizen Planning Academy model of public outreach and education. *Journal of Planning Education and Research*, 35(2), pp 174–87.

Marohn, C.L. (2021) *Confessions of a Recovering Engineer: The Strong Towns Vision for Transportation in the Next American City*, Hoboken, New Jersey: Wiley.

Marshall, W.E. and Ferenchak, N.N. (2020) Authors' response to the letter to the editor regarding why cities with high bicycling rates are safer for all road users. *Journal of Transport & Health*, 16, 100677, DOI: 10.1016/j.jth.2019.100677.

Martin, M.E., Swanlund, D., and Schuurman, N. (2023) Problems with quantitative categorization: an argument for qualitative approaches. *Environment and Planning F*, 2(3), DOI: 10.1177/26349825231163140.

Mattern, S. (2015) Mission control: a history of the urban dashboard. *Places Journal* [online], Available from: https://placesjournal.org/article/mission-control-a-history-of-the-urban-dashboard/.

Mbembe, A. (2021) *Out of the Dark Night: Essays on Decolonization*, New York: Columbia University Press.

McConnell, C.L. (2014) *Digital Inclusion and Techno-Capital in Austin, Texas*, Austin, TX: The University of Texas at Austin.

McGrath, B. (1989) Problems of setting up an urban planning system in The Gambia. *Cities*, 6(4), pp 325–35.

McKenzie, G. (2019) Spatiotemporal comparative analysis of scooter-share and bike-share usage patterns in Washington, DC. *Journal of Transport Geography*, 78(May), pp 19–28.

McNeil, N., Broach, J., and Dill, J. (2018) Breaking barriers to bike share: lessons on bike share equity. *ITE Journal (Institute of Transportation Engineers)*, 88(2), pp 31–5.

Melia, D.S. (2019) Why did UK governments cut road building in the 1990s and expand it after 2010? *Transport Policy*, 81, pp 242–53.

Melia, S. (2020) Learning critical realist research by example: political decision-making in transport. *Journal of Critical Realism*, 19(3), pp 285–303.

Meyer, E. (2019) New colonialism in developmental aid. *Paideia*, 6(1) [online], Available from: https://digitalcommons.calpoly.edu/paideia/vol6/iss1/18.

Meyer, M.D. (2016) Public participation and engagement. In: *Transportation Planning Handbook*, Hoboken, NJ: Wiley, pp 1111–56.

Miller, H.J. (2004) Tobler's First Law and spatial analysis. *Annals of the Association of American Geographers*, 94(2), pp 284–9.

Mitlin, D. (2008) With and beyond the state—co-production as a route to political influence, power and transformation for grassroots organizations. *Environment and Urbanization*, 20(2), pp 339–60.

Morgan, D.L. (2014) Pragmatism as a paradigm for social research. *Qualitative Inquiry*, 20(8), pp 1045–53.

Mumford, L. (1963) *The Highway and the City*, New York: Harcourt, Brace, Jovanovich.

Mumford, L. (1964) Authoritarian and democratic technics. *Technology and Culture*, 5(1), pp 1–8.

Murray, D.J. (2005) A critical analysis of communicative rationality as a theoretical underpinning for collaborative approaches to integrated resource and environmental management. *Environments*, 33(2), pp 17–34.

NACTO (2014) *NACTO Urban Bikeway Design Guide* (2nd edn), Washington, DC: Island Press.

Næss, P. (2015) Critical realism, urban planning and urban research. *European Planning Studies*, 23(6), pp 1228–44.

Næss, P. (2016) Built environment, causality and urban planning. *Planning Theory & Practice*, 17(1), pp 52–71.

Næss, P. and Strand, A. (2012) What kinds of traffic forecasts are possible? *Journal of Critical Realism*, 11(3), pp 277–95.

Neilson, A., Indratmo, D.B., and Tjandra, S. (2019) Systematic review of the literature on big data in the transportation domain: concepts and applications. *Big Data Research*, 17, pp 35–44.

Noland, R.B. (2007) Transport planning and environmental assessment: implications of induced travel effects. *International Journal of Sustainable Transportation*, 1(1), pp 1–28.

Okoli, C. and Pawlowski, S.D. (2004) The Delphi method as a research tool: an example, design considerations and applications. *Information & Management*, 42(1), pp 15–29.

Okolo, A.L. and Akwu, J.O. (2016) China's foreign direct investment in Africa's land: hallmarks of neo-colonialism or South–South cooperation? *Africa Review*, 8(1), pp 44–59.

OPEC Fund (2023) Banjul Airport Rehabilitation Project (Phase II), OPEC Fund for International Development [online], Available from: https://opecfund.org/operations/list/banjul-airport-rehabilitation-project-phase-ii.

Ortúzar, J. de D. and Willumsen, L.G. (2011) *Modelling Transport*, Chichester: Wiley.

Pak, B., Chua, A., and Vande Moere, A. (2017) FixMyStreet Brussels: socio-demographic inequality in crowdsourced civic participation. *Journal of Urban Technology*, 24(2), 65–87.

Panjwani, H. (2022) Here's where candidates for Austin mayor stand on three big issues. KUT Radio, Austin's NPR Station [online] October 6, Available from: https://www.kut.org/politics/2022-10-06/heres-where-candidates-for-austin-mayor-stand-on-three-big-issues.

Peng, P., Yang, Y., Lu, F., Cheng, S., Mou, N., and Yang, R. (2018) Modelling the competitiveness of the ports along the Maritime Silk Road with big data. *Transportation Research Part A: Policy and Practice*, 118(October), pp 852–67.

Peng, Z.-R., Lu, K.-F., Liu, Y., and Zhai, W. (2023) The pathway of urban planning AI: from planning support to plan-making. *Journal of Planning Education and Research*. DOI: 10.1177/0739456X231180568.

Pereira, R.H.M.M., Schwanen, T., and Banister, D. (2017) Distributive justice and equity in transportation. *Transport Reviews*, 37(2), pp 170–91.

Pew Research Center (2016) 13% of Americans don't use the internet. Who are they? [online], Available from: http://www.pewresearch.org/fact-tank/2016/09/07/some-americans-dont-use-the-internet-who-are-they/.

Rahim Taleqani, A., Hough, J., and Nygard, K.E. (2019) Public opinion on dockless bike sharing: a machine learning approach. *Transportation Research Record: Journal of the Transportation Research Board*, 2673(4), pp 195–204.

Reconnect Austin (2022) *Reconnect Austin* [online], Available from: https://reconnectaustin.com/.

Republic of The Gambia (2018) *Youth and Trade Roadmap of The Gambia, 2018–2022, Tourism Sector*. Bakau, The Gambia: International Trade Centre.

Rethink35 (2023) The Rethink35 Plan – Austin, Texas Freeway Removal Proposal [online], Available from: https://rethink35.org/the-rethink35-plan.

Rethink35, Texas Public Interest Research Group, and Environment Texas (2022) Rethink et al. v. TxDOT et al., CIVIL ACTION NO. 1-cv-22-00620 [online], Available from: https://www.documentcloud.org/documents/23307503-rethink-35-lawsuit.

Rid, W., Ezeuduji, I.O., and Pröbstl-Haider, U. (2014) Segmentation by motivation for rural tourism activities in The Gambia. *Tourism Management*, 40, pp 102–16.

Ride Report (2023) Global Micromobility Dashboard [online], Available from: https://public.ridereport.com

Riggs, W. (2022) *End of The Road: Reimagining The Street as The Heart of The City*, Bristol: Bristol University Press.

Rose, G. (1997) Situating knowledges: positionality, reflexivities and other tactics. *Progress in Human Geography*, 21(3), pp 305–20.

Rosenbloom, S. and Pleissis-Fraissard, M. (2010) Women's travel in developed and developing countries: two versions of the same story? In: *Women's Issues in Transportation: Summary of the 4th International Conference, Volume 1: Conference Overview and Plenary Papers* [online], Available from: https://www.nap.edu/catalog/22901.

Rothstein, R. (2017) *The Color of Law: A Forgotten History of How Our Government Segregated America*, New York: Liveright.

Roy, A. and Nelson, T. (2018) Bias correction in geolocated crowdsourced data from Strava using Machine Learning based linear models. *Geophysical Research Abstracts* [online], Available from: https://ui.adsabs.harvard.edu/abs/2018EGUGA..2010983R/abstract.

Roy, A., Fuller, D., Stanley, K., and Nelson, T. (2020) Classifying transport mode from global positioning systems and accelerometer data: a machine learning approach. *Findings* [online], Available from: https://findingspress.org/article/14520-classifying-transport-mode-from-global-positioning-systems-and-accelerometer-data-a-machine-learning-approach.

Runde, J. and de Rond, M. (2010) Evaluating causal explanations of specific events. *Organization Studies*, 31(4), pp 431–50.

Sager, T. (2006) The logic of critical communicative planning: transaction cost alteration. *Planning Theory*, 5(3), pp 223–54.

Saldaña, J. (2016) *The Coding Manual for Qualitative Researchers*, Thousand Oaks, CA: Sage.

Saldaña, S. and Greenfield, A. (2023) Why a group opposing the planned I-35 expansion in Austin dropped its environmental lawsuit. Texas Standard [online], Available from: https://www.texasstandard.org/stories/rethin k35-drops-environmental-lawsuit-txdot-over-interstate-35-expansion-aus tin-tx/.

Sanchez, T. (2023) *Planning With Artificial Intelligence*, American Planning Association [online], Available from: https://www.planning.org/publicati ons/report/9270237/.

Sandoval, G. (2007) Catalytic Gaze: Co-evolutionary Adaptation in an Emerging New Mesoamerican Neighborhood in Los Angeles. Berkeley Planning Journal [online], Available from: https://escholarship.org/cont ent/qt3tm7q153/qt3tm7q153_noSplash_76f5b908de4e5175843b54c62 d5548fd.pdf?t=poq2dg.

Saudi Fund for Development (2022) Saudi Fund for Development marks the completion of the $31 million Banjul International Airport project in The Gambia [online], Available from: https://www.sfd.gov.sa/en/n173.

Sayer, R.A. (2000) *Realism and Social Science*, Thousand Oaks, CA: Sage.

Schimek, P. (2020) Comment on *Why cities with high bicycling rates are safer for all road users. Journal of Transport & Health* 16, p 100676 [online], Available from: https://www.sciencedirect.com/science/article/abs/pii/S221414051 9305481?via%3Dihub.

Schively, C. (2007) Understanding the NIMBY and LULU phenomena: reassessing our knowledge base and informing future research. *Journal of Planning Literature*, 21(3), pp 255–66.

Schweitzer, L.A. (2014) Planning and social media: a case study of public transit and stigma on Twitter. *Journal of the American Planning Association*, 80(3), pp 218–38.

Shearmur, R. (2015) Dazzled by data: big data, the census and urban geography. *Urban Geography*, 36(7), pp 965–68.

Silveira-Santos, T., Manuel Vassallo, J., and Torres, E. (2022) Using machine learning models to predict the willingness to carry lightweight goods by bike and kick-scooter. *Transportation Research Interdisciplinary Perspectives*, 13, 100568, DOI: 10.1016/j.trip.2022.100568.

Simpson, E.H. (1951) The interpretation of interaction in contingency tables. *Journal of the Royal Statistical Society: Series B (Methodological)*, 13(2), pp 238–41.

Söderberg f.k.a. Andersson, A., Adell, E. and Winslott Hiselius, L. (2021) What is the substitution effect of e-bikes? A randomised controlled trial. *Transportation Research Part D: Transport and Environment*, 90, 102648, DOI: 10.1016/j.trd.2020.102648.

Stewart, A.F., Zegras, P.C., Tinn, P., and Rosenblum, J.L. (2018) Tangible tools for public transportation planning: public involvement and learning for bus rapid transit corridor design. *Transportation Research Record: Journal of the Transportation Research Board*, 2672(4): DOI: 10.1177/ 036119811879746.

Streetmix (2023) *Streetmix*. July 5 [online], Available from: https://street mix.net/.

Sui, D., Goodchild, M., and Elwood, S. (2013) Volunteered geographic information, the Exaflood, and the growing digital divide. In: D. Sui, S. Elwood, and M. Goodchild (eds) *Crowdsourcing Geographic Knowledge: Volunteered Geographic Information in Theory and Practice*, New York: Springer, pp 1–14.

Sun, B., Appiah, J., and Park, B.B. (2020) Practical guidance for using mesoscopic simulation tools, *Transportation Research Procedia: Recent Advances and Emerging Issues in Transport Research – An Editorial Note for the Selected Proceedings of WCTR 2019 Mumbai*, 48, pp 764–76.

Taylor, L. (2016) No place to hide? The ethics and analytics of tracking mobility using mobile phone data. *Environment and Planning D: Society and Space*, 34(2), pp 319–36.

Taylor, S.D. (2018) Africa and foreign direct investment. In: S.O. Oloruntoba and T. Falola (eds) *The Palgrave Handbook of African Politics, Governance and Development*, New York, Palgrave Macmillan US, pp 709–22.

Texas A&M Transportation Institute (n.d.) Texas A&M Transportation Institute 70 years of innovation [online], Available from: https://tti.tamu. edu/about/history/.

Texas A&M Transportation Institute (2021) 100 most congested roadways in Texas 2021 [online], Available from: https://mobility.tamu.edu/texas-most-congested-roadways/.

Texas Public Interest Research Group (2022) Lawsuit challenges proposed I-35 highway expansions in Austin, [online] August 4, Available from: https://web.archive.org/web/20220804004712/https://texpirg.org/news/txp/lawsuit-challenges-proposed-i-35-highway-expansions-austin.

Thompson, K. (2023) 'Completely unacceptable': Austin group slams final I-35 plan. What TxDOT says. KXAN Austin, [online] August 22, Available from: https://www.kxan.com/news/local/austin/completely-unaccepta ble-austin-group-slams-final-i-35-plan-what-txdot-says/.

Thorpe, A. (2017) Rethinking participation, rethinking planning. *Planning Theory and Practice*, 18(4), pp 566–82.

Tinsley, M. (2021) Towards a postcolonial critical realism. *Critical Sociology*, 48(2), DOI: 10.1177/08969205211003962.

Tironi, M. and Valderrama, M. (2018) Unpacking a citizen self-tracking device: smartness and idiocy in the accumulation of cycling mobility data. *Environment and Planning D: Society and Space*, 36(2), pp 294–312.

Tobler, W.R. (1970) A computer movie simulating urban growth in the Detroit region. *Economic Geography*, 46 (Supplement: Proceedings of the International Geographical Union, Commission on Quantitative Methods, June 1970), pp 234–40.

TxDOT (2011) My35: I-35 Corridor Advisory Committee Plan [online], Available from: https://ftp.txdot.gov/pub/txdot-info/my35/advisory_plan.pdf.

TxDOT (2019) National Environmental Policy Act (NEPA) Assignment Documentation [online], Available from: https://www.txdot.gov/content/txdotreimagine/us/en/home/about/programs/environmental/nepa-assignment-documentation.html.

TxDOT (2020) Purpose and Need Draft Technical Report [online], Available from: https://my35capex.com/wp-content/uploads/2020/10/Draft-Purpose-Need-Technical-Report_VSM1.pdf.

TxDOT (2022) I-35 Capital Express Central [online], Available from: https://my35capex.com/projects/i-35-capital-express-central/.

TxDOT (2023a) I-35 Capital Express Central Project – Draft Environmental Impact Statement and Public Hearing Materials [online], Available from: https://my35capex.com/draft-eis/.

TxDOT (2023b) I-35 Capital Express North – Capital Express [online], Available from: https://my35capex.com/projects/i-35-capital-express-north/.

TxDOT (2023c) I-35 Capital Express South – Capital Express [online], Available from: https://my35capex.com/projects/i-35-capital-express-south/.

TxDOT (2023d) Traffic Count Maps [online], Available from: http://txdot.gov/en/home/data-maps/traffic-count-maps.html.

US Department of Transportation (2022a) Climate action [online], Available from: https://www.transportation.gov/priorities/climate-and-sustainability/climate-action.

US Department of Transportation (2022b) Promising practices for meaningful public involvement in transportation decision-making [online], Available from: https://www.transportation.gov/priorities/equity/promising-practices-meaningful-public-involvement-transportation-decision-making.

US Federal Highway Administration (2023) Travel Model Improvement Program [online], Available from: https://tmip.org/.

Voulgaris, C. (2020) What is a forecast for? Motivations for transit ridership forecast accuracy in the federal New Starts program. *Journal of the American Planning Association*, 86(4), pp 458–69.

Wachs, M. (1990) Ethics and advocacy in forecasting for public policy. *Business & Professional Ethics Journal*, 9(1), pp 141–57.

Wachs, M. (2001) Forecasting versus envisioning: a new window on the future. *Journal of the American Planning Association*, 67(4), pp 367–72.

Waite, D. (2022) Critical realist perspectives on the urban growth system. *Environment and Planning A: Economy and Space*, 54(6), pp 1219–35.

Walsh, D. and Evans, K. (2014) Critical realism: an important theoretical perspective for midwifery research. *Midwifery*, 30(1), pp e1–6.

Watson, V. (2014) Co-production and collaboration in planning – the difference. *Planning Theory & Practice*, 15(1), pp 62–76.

Wear, B. (2007) Toll road plan cruises onward. Austin American-Statesman, October 9, p A01.

Wear, B. (2016) Lone Star Rail officially dead after final CAMPO vote. Austin American-Statesman [online] October 18, Available from: https://www.statesman.com/story/news/2016/10/18/lone-star-rail-officially-dead-after-final-campo-vote/10000086007/.

Weeg, W. (1946) City Council agrees to buy super highway right-of-way. Austin Statesman, September.

Weiner, E. (1997) Urban Transportation Planning in the United States: An Historical Overview [online], Available from: https://rosap.ntl.bts.gov/view/dot/13691.

Wilson, P.A. (1997) Building social capital: a learning agenda for the twenty-first century. *Urban Studies*, 34(512), pp 745–60.

Witmer, J. (2021) Simpson's Paradox, visual displays, and causal diagrams. *The American Mathematical Monthly*, 128(7), pp 598–610.

World Bank (2011) *Africa Region Tourism Strategy: Transformation through Tourism – Harnessing Tourism for Growth and Improved Livelihoods* Washington, DC: World Bank [online], Available from: http://hdl.handle.net/10986/12841.

World Bank (2021) World Bank Climate Change Knowledge Portal [online], Available from: https://climateknowledgeportal.worldbank.org/.

World Bank (2022) World Bank open data [online], Available from: https://data.worldbank.org.

Wray, J.H. (2008) *Pedal Power: The Quiet Rise of the Bicycle in American Public Life*, Boulder, CO: Paradigm Publishers.

Wright, S. (2022) In praise of the humble sidewalk, *Planning*, Spring [online], Available from: https://www.planning.org/planning/2022/spring/in-praise-of-the-humble-sidewalk/.

Wu, H., Avner, P., Boisjoly, G., Braga, C.K.V., El-Geneidy, A., Huang, J. et al (2021) Urban access across the globe: an international comparison of different transport modes. *NPJ Urban Sustainability*, 1(1), DOI: 10.1038/s42949-021-00020-2.

Wu, L., Gu, W., Fan, W., and Cassidy, M.J. (2020) Optimal design of transit networks fed by shared bikes. *Transportation Research Part B: Methodological*, 131, pp 63–83.

Wyly, E. (2014) The new quantitative revolution. *Dialogues in Human Geography*, 4(1), pp 26–38.

Zachariadis, M., Scott, S., and Barrett, M. (2013) Methodological implications of critical realism for mixed-methods research. *MIS Quarterly*, 37(3), pp 855–79.

Zhu, X., Ory, M.G., Xu, M., Towne, S.D. Jr, Lu, Z., Hammond, T. et al (2022) Physical activity impacts of an activity-friendly community: a natural experiment study protocol. *Frontiers in Public Health*, 10 [online], Available from: https://www.frontiersin.org/articles/10.3389/fpubh.2022.929331.

Index